BALANCING YOUR BEST SELF

By

Nancy Zimmerman

Hedgehog Hill Press

An imprint of S & Z Unlimited

S & Z Unlimited
P.O. Box 2380
Anderson, IN 46018

sandzunlimited.com

A Hedgehog Hill Press original, 2016

Cover by Rebekah Raffield

ISBN 978-0692536933

Non-Fiction

Previous books in the "Living Your Best Life" series:

Embracing Your Best Self

Confronting Your Best Self

Fiction

with co-author Arthur L. Shead

Flashmob

Annie's Diaries

DEDICATION

I am dedicating this to my friends, past and present, who have allowed me into their lives..... whether I was balanced or not. Thank you all for contributing to the tapestry of my life. Namaste.

INTRODUCTION

After experiencing a set of circumstances that resulted in an awareness and a spiritual awakening, I wrote my first book, EMBRACING YOUR BEST SELF. I thought since I was more aware and made more conscious choices, that enlightenment would just naturally lead to a much more fulfilling life. It did not work quite that way. I lost a bit of the focus I had and found myself floundering with choices and feelings. I realized that I needed to confront, yet even more thoroughly, issues that I thought had been resolved. This resulted in the writing of my second book, CONFRONTING YOUR BEST SELF. It was when the book was being edited that my editor, as an observer, pointed out that I talked a lot about confronting issues but there seemed to be a hole with something left out, a problem that had not been confronted, that led to my feelings of disconnect. After thinking about this, I was able to pinpoint what he was talking about and address it. It was when I was about 80% finished with this book that I realized the problems I was encountering were nothing more than an imbalance between my thoughts and feelings and my actions regarding those thoughts and feelings. I had lost my sense of balance. When I recognized this "hole", I realized that there would be a third book that needed to be written, and therefore, I am beginning this book, BALANCING YOUR BEST SELF.

All of my books are available through Amazon and they are available on Kindle also. If you wish to interact with me, my e-mail address is nancy@sandzunlimited.com and I would be happy to help you in any way possible. I am also beginning to set up my current calendar and will be available for speaking engagements. I am excited about how my life has changed in the past three years and I know that everyone can find their very Best Self. Enjoy.

PART ONE

WHAT DO WE NEED TO BALANCE?

This book is going to be more hands-on than the other two books. It is not necessary that you have read the other two books for this to be helpful, but it will sometimes refer to ideas that were expressed in those books. The best way to embrace this book is with an open mind. Some of the suggestions that will be made are probably out of your comfort zone only because they may encourage you to think a bit differently than you currently do about some issues.

When we begin our discussion on balance, we usually think of a seesaw, with a mid-point balancing one side against the other. For our discussion on balance, I am going to have you think about those entertainers that take a plate and start spinning it on a rod and keep adding another plate on another rod. When the first plate begins to wobble, they quickly go back and give it another spin. They keep adding plates and rods and going back and spinning those that begin to wobble. This illustration is more in tune to the way we find the balancing in our lives. We never have just one issue with two sides. We have multiple issues with many different ways of looking at each issue. Keeping many plates spinning at the same time is a much different kind of balance than the balance we find on a seesaw.

To balance on a seesaw it is only necessary to balance the weight on each end. If there are two unequal weights, one can just be moved forward more in order to keep the length/weight ratio even. It is a trial and error effort. Many situations are just as easily balanced in life. We become very adept at dealing with the minor, day -to- day, and issues so that they rarely become problematic. These issues are often akin to juggling our work schedule with a doctor's appointment, or, perhaps, finding a time to shop for groceries or get other errands done. They require balancing, but we don't even consider it a balancing act because it has become so commonplace for us.

The kind of balance that will help us confront and embrace our best selves is one of a mind-body-spirit balance. The very titles of my first two books indicate a direction, in and of itself. While embracing someone, we open our arms and draw someone toward us. When we consider confronting, we face a conflict and something that serves to separate us. Balance shows us that regardless of the number of points whether on a line or a circle requires a touching of many points along that line to keep the equilibrium. Balance is necessary throughout life.

We can look at our life in two ways. We can look at as a trip from point A to point B. We see our birth as point A and our death as point B. If that line were represented by a string, we would start at point A and as we went further from that point, we would need to either pull the string tighter or we would need to find ways to prop the string so that it would not drag onto the ground. If we are propping the string, there will be times when the props are taller than other times and we have the undulating hills and valleys referred to in life.

We can also look at life as a circle. When we do that, we have no beginning and no end. We are represented as an eternal constantly spiraling life. You will find no beginning and no end. When we have this approach to life, we require stabilizers all along to keep the circle balanced. It would be rather like a hula hoop continually needing to be readjusted in order to keep it spinning.

It doesn't really matter which view we consider for the stretch of life. What does matter is that whichever diagram we choose to represent our lives we recognize the need for balance. When we balance our lives, we do not eliminate the hills and valleys; we moderate them so that they do not cause us serious problems and so that we can lead the best life possible. When we are leading the best life possible we are able to be our best self and we will experience a life full of joy.

MEDITATION, JOURNALING, AND OTHER TOOLS

Meditation, for our purposes, is going to refer to establishing any practice that will enable us to quiet our minds and thoughts. When we quiet our thoughts and our minds we are more adequately able to make conscious choices that will help us balance our lives. Some of your reading this already have a spiritual practice of meditation in your day with which you are very comfortable. If you do, then you already know the benefits it can bring to your consciousness. If you have never established any meditation practices, I will offer several tips along the way that will help you ease into the practice and show you the benefits. It will be your choice at that time to decide if the practice will help you achieve balance in your life. We need to remember that meditation is not something we need in order to control our thoughts, it is something we need so that our thoughts do not control us.

Current scientific research is showing us that the act of coloring can have the same benefits for us that traditional forms of meditation carries. It is something that I find very interesting and I purchased some coloring books myself to see if there is a relaxing element that will take us to the same introspective place that meditation does.

Journaling, in the sense we will use it here, will be a simple matter of buying an attractive blank book that will serve as a repository for thoughts, feelings, and ideas that you encounter on this journey. Like meditation practices, some of you have written in a journal for years and have found it to be a benefit in your life. If so, you will continue this because you have learned the value for you. If, like me, you have not made this a regular practice, you can still use it in a productive way to help when you feel a need to perhaps sort through thoughts and feelings that are causing you angst. I do not journal daily but I do make notations of quotes and thoughts that I find helpful. That is what works for me and as we concentrate on finding our balance, you will have to decide what works for you.

Make your journaling relaxed and realize that life is not a sprint, it is an exercise in finding the tools and how to use them in a way that allows you to relax and enjoy the life you are living.

Yoga and exercise are also tools that may be used to help balance your best self. Meditation provides a spiritual tool, journaling provides a mental tool, and yoga and exercise provide a physical balance. We are spiritual beings but we agreed to contain ourselves in this "pod" we call our body. One of the most wonderful things about this body for most of us is the mobility that it affords us. To be balanced in the mind/body/spirit way, we need to honor our body and give it the exercise it needs to keep it as mobile as possible.

We will find that these practices, like any other tools in our arsenal, are only as helpful as we allow them to be. A dishcloth does not wash dishes by itself. It only helps wash dishes when we use it. Same with a dust cloth, a vacuum cleaner, or a lawn rake. They are helpers available to us when we decide a particular chore needs some attention.

There are other tools we use that help us achieve a balance in our life. These tools include things like music, art, hobbies, and nature. We will use all sorts of items that will draw us into different ways of thinking and different ways of looking at life. There will be times that we are going to get out of our comfort zones so that we can understand what will get us into balance, perhaps for the first time in our lives. Some of what we try may be beneficial for some of us and some may not be helpful at all. Know right now, that there are no definite answers given in this book for a "cure" of any sorts. We are all on a personal journey and that journey demands of us our total involvement with ourselves. There is no right or wrong in our approach, I am only giving you my suggestions. As you read this book, I hope you feel free to get in touch with me and establish a dialogue that will help us both. I can be reached by e-mail at nancy@sandzunlimited.com   and will look forward to any input and conversation. I can be found on Facebook at www.facebook/Embracing Your Best Self and look forward to adding you to this growing support system.

To give you an idea of how these tools can help you, I will share how I use these techniques. I use meditation techniques when I am immersing myself in nature. It occurs when I am sitting outside on a summer night looking up in the sky observing the stars. It happens when I am petting a kitten or when I am looking at a snowy day. Any time I take myself away from any thought to a place of no thought, I am involved in meditation. I journal when I need to settle the thoughts I am having. I use the journaling for affirmations and I also use it to make notations of quotes that I find particularly helpful. I am very sporadic in my efforts at physical exercise. That is where the weak point of my balance is. I have accepted the necessity of balance in the spiritual and the mental, but in most phases of life, I have been lax in addressing the physical.   Issues that have caused me problems, therefore, are mostly of a physical nature because that is where I have given less attention to the need for balance.   I have issues dealing with weight and body flexibility. Addressing the balance needed with the physical aspects of myself will help me get closer to my best self. You, too, may find some techniques come more naturally than others.

One of the greatest tools that I have found is the connection I have with those who are also thinking and reacting to a new consciousness. It is in our awareness that we achieve the enlightenment that leads us to a conscious awakening. Once we get to this point, we are reaching our best selves and we find that there are many who truly do not understand our new way of thinking. We then really crave conversation with others who understand us. We have given up the ego's need to make everyone think our way of thinking is the best; we only want to be able to express ourselves freely without censorship.

One of the first exercises that I would suggest, and one I am working on myself is establishing a playlist of tunes that help me express myself at the highest emotional level. Some of these songs are so beautiful to me that they bring me to tears. Some of them draw upon songs that meant something to me and another person who is no longer in my life. Some of them help me recall beautiful memories. Some of them are just songs that help me recall a quieter time in my life before I experienced heartache and disappointment. The emotion we are hoping to evoke is one of joy, not sadness. While some of the songs we choose may be a bit bittersweet, they still will bring a passion to our life in some way. This is an exercise that is ongoing because there may be some new song that just has lyrics or chords in it that cause our hearts to swell. Choose any songs you want that will call upon your passion.

I find myself using the word "passion" more often than I ever have. I want passion in my life again. It is there when we are young, usually too young to remember. We find it when we watch toddlers play. We forget that passion is how we started life and passion is the purpose of life. We listen to the messages that others send us and absorb them and before we know it, we lose our passion. Then, perhaps, we find another person who sparks a passion within us. We link

the term passion to this person and begin to feel that
when we are with this person we have passion and
when we are not with this person, we do not have
passion. Passion then becomes dependent upon
someone else in our minds. This is an imbalance. We
can find passion daily if we choose. We can live
passionately, regardless of our circumstances. We live
passionately when we engage with ourselves on a
moment to moment basis. We live a passionate life
when we live every moment in a vibrant state of
pleasure with life itself. Passion exists within us.
Passion, once found, can be radiated when we engage
with others who also live passionate lives.

HOW DID I KNOW I WAS OUT OF BALANCE?

I realized how out of balance I was in my own life when I was writing my second book. I was confronting issues I thought were behind me. Some of those issues were more difficult to uncover than others. Some of those issues were body/size issues that I have had for as long as I can remember. I lost about 150 pounds because I escaped my fears of how I presented myself and replaced them with a passion to be smaller to accommodate spending time with my new grandson. I let the love for my grandson overrule the love for food. I let that love fill up the empty spaces in my life that I was trying to fill with food. I thought that because I was no longer eating processed foods, drinking carbonated sodas, and making many other dietary changes that this new body would become my norm. I would look in the mirror and even though my clothing size was one I was pleased with, my body was far from it. I was a 63 -year-old woman whose skin had been stretched to the limit for 20 years. The elasticity of a twenty- year- old was not possible and the folds of loose skin did not please me. I did not love my body. I did not accept my body. It became a battleground for me yet again. As I struggled with the size, I found my clothes once again getting tight then not fitting at all. I reached a panic mode and realized I had learned nothing spiritually if I was allowing these fears to send me over the edge. Other insecurities began rearing their ugly head and then the good old Ego had to put in its two cents worth.

I began listening to the Ego retelling all of the old messages I thought I had resolved through spiritual awakening. I rationalized my behaviors and went back to the old Scarlett O'Hara mode that, "I will think about that tomorrow." The more panicky I became, the more outside issues would bother me. I began to dwell on issues of a global significance and no longer focused on local ways that I could help those around me and make a difference in the lives of others. My focus was so far off that my balance was thrown into a tailspin.

I finished my book with a renewed appreciation of the necessity of not only getting back into balance but also in finding a way to stay in balance. That is the intention of this book. I am writing it so that anyone who reads it can find a way to balance their thoughts successfully so that the circumstances we desire are drawn to us.

We can recognize that we are out of balance when we find that many of our days are spent in turmoil and conflict. When our life doesn't seem to be working quite like we would think it should, we can see the need for some balance of some kind. The achievement of balance will come when we decide where we will put our focus. When my focus changed, my balance was off. It is not always easy to regain that focus, but it isn't as difficult as we usually make it out to be. A beginning point to regain your balance and your direction is to take the time to look at different areas in your life that are causing you grief. Let us say you are experiencing relationship difficulties of some kind (family, love, work, etc.). What is bothering you about these relationships? Don't be afraid to use journaling and write all of this down, because it will help you to keep focused. Sometimes we have to realize that what is causing us angst may not even be on someone else's radar. They might very well not be aware there is a problem for you because there is no problem for them. That is very often the case. We also have to realize, if we are really wanting to regain balance, that sometimes we create our own turmoil just to create our own tension. I am not certain why humans do this, but we do. It is much akin to the sand that gets into an oyster and causes it to constantly secrete a substance around it so that it will not be so irritating. Unfortunately for us, the result is not so soothing nor is it as beautiful as the resultant pearl is to the oyster.

Another point that is necessary if we are wanting to get our life back into balance is to realize that we are only working on ourselves. We will not achieve balance if we think that it will happen when others change to accommodate us. Not. Going. To. Happen. Balance only occurs for us all when we look at our issues of conflict with fresh eyes. We should not be out to change others. The good news is that we often don't have to change ourselves either to achieve balance. We can achieve balance by realizing that changing where we are focusing can be a bit like bringing a camera into focus. Just a slight turn can bring us from fuzzy to clear. Thinking that we have to overhaul ourselves and become someone in a different skin by making many changes can be a bit daunting, and it would be self-defeating. We are exactly who we are intended to be, no exceptions. The only reason we look for a balance in our lives is to make OUR life more easily navigated, not for any other reason. If we enjoy being off balance, then there is no reason to read any further. Our lives just operate on a much higher frequency with much more ease and enjoyment when we are balanced.

ALL YA NEED IS LOVE

Poems have been written and songs have been sung about love. We all need it and we all have it to give. The way we give love indicates our ability to receive it. I have struggled with love or the lack of love as long as I can remember and I am not sure why there is such a deficit.

I was born to a thirty-three year old mother and a thirty-two year old father in 1949. It was shortly after the war had ended (WWII) and I was a member of the Baby Boomer generation. I am not sure if there was anything of any significance that happened to me during my early years because I remember none of that time. I have cute stories told about some of my interactions with family members, but I did not see many affectionate pictures of me with my parents. I always remember having a panic when I was in a group of people wanting to keep my mother in sight for fear that she might forget I was around and go off without me. When I was an adult and we would laugh about this, I always asked if she had ever forgotten me anywhere that would have led to this feeling. She didn't remember a time, but somehow I held that feeling. I have never understood why I felt this way and it never made a great deal of sense because I always had an independent streak that wanted to get out and away from home as I went into the college years.

I had a sister who was three and a half years younger and we were never close that I can recall. We shared a room, but that was the extent of our closeness, and we pretty well had our areas assigned to us so that we knew exactly where our domain was in that room. The only time that we shared friends was when I had moved out and visited some of her high school friends when they were freshmen. That was when I met a friend of hers who I would later marry. We shared a group of friends for several years then she met her husband and went a different direction. These friends and I still share memories and keep in touch with. I always found it amazing that so many sisters were friends because even when we shared this group of friends, she and I weren't friends with each other as much as we either one were with all of the others.

I think my mother had always hoped we would be friends, but it just never did quite happen and I gave up on that idea years ago. I still talk to her occasionally but she has never confided in me like I understand many younger sisters do with their older sisters. I have never had this closeness so it is not something I miss as much as it is something I regret never having. It would have been nice, I think.

When I started school, I was able to read and do basic math already so it was determined that even though I was only six years old, I would be taken out of the first grade and put into the second grade about two weeks after school started. I had already made some friends and had a teacher I liked and was taken from a pleasant room to a sea of older faces and a teacher who had a perpetual scowl on her face. The only socializing I had done had been very brief and to go into a situation that involved seven and eight year olds was scary. I remember thinking that it would be okay if I could just play with my friends from the first grade at recess but they played at a different place in the playground and I was not allowed to go there since I was in the second grade. The new classmates did not like it that some little kid was invading their space. It did not help that this was a small country school where everyone knew everyone else. The second grade classroom also had a shared third grade. Part of the third grade was in that room and part was in the fourth grade. I was also a "chunky" six year old so naturally add that to immature and I was fodder for the name calling. That was my introduction to friendships.

Looking at these brief scenarios you can see that there were insecurities about myself from the beginning of my time on this earth. When we are young we come into the world with no preformed ideas. The world is our oyster, but our experiences shape who we become. While I did not sense that I was ever mistreated like we consider actual mistreatment, I was not nurtured with love. I was clothed, fed, and housed. I was disciplined when it was felt I needed to be disciplined. I don't know if I was ever held and hugged just because I was loved. I truly remember more aggravation and correction than I do affection in my life. That is a memory when I begin to realize now how much I didn't have in the way of love as I was young. As I consider this, however, I also have to understand that I was raised in a time when sharing our thoughts and feelings was not encouraged. I understand why it is difficult for me to see a grown woman who deserves to be loved when I was not even a cute little girl who deserved love. I know now that love is what we are, and not what we deserve. This is a mental perception and not an emotional one. The emotional little girl who feels like she is on the outside looking in remains with me to this day. This little girl is still trying to fill up the space where love should reign with food. It will never be enough. She needs to learn to love herself and that will come when she learns to balance her life.

As I grew up, I always felt that love was conditional. If I was well-behaved, I was loved. If I misbehaved or embarrassed my mother, I would be corrected and love would be withheld. This may or may not be a perception that anyone else around me would have gathered from my interaction with my parents but it is at the core of how my life felt. Our feelings are primary in gaining an understanding of the world around us. How we feel is primary in how we react and how we react is what forms our point of attraction to what comes to us in life.

While growing up, I had a general feeling that whatever I did was not good enough. A feeling that I was not good enough. It would stand to reason that I have had commitment issues. I never have felt like anyone could commit to me so I have inadvertently sought relationships that could never have withstood the test of time. **This is an important concept. We draw to us that which we think and feel that we deserve.** I had several relationships that I found out many years later were with gay men, one of which I married. Then there were the men who had girlfriend or wives and wanted a relationship with me also. They were safe for me because they could not commit any more than I could, I would never have been called upon to commit to them. I was safe for them because somewhere at the level of both of our souls, we knew that commitment would never be the issue. The sad part of those situations is that they only continued to reinforce within me the message that I was not good enough. It has been only recently that I have realized that there was something deep within me that would call me to be attracted to a man who did not want to commit to a woman and that something was a fear of commitment. The fear was greater than I had ever realized. I had a horrific fear of unreturned love. That fear was so great that amazingly I sought out the most unavailable people on the planet, people who would turn me away and prove that I was unlovable. My greatest fear was what I continually drew to me.

When we begin recognizing patterns we are more able to realize areas where we need balance. While I have not yet been able to make a lifetime commitment in a romantic relationship, it does not hold true that I cannot commit love to a relationship. I have had friends that I have loved through the years and still interact with and think about often. I have had love for pets, and yes, that counts. Animals are often some of the first sentient beings we interact with in a loving way. Having and caring for a pet is one of the first ways we teach children the responsibility involved in a nurturing relationship. I have also had the love for my children and grandchildren. There are all sorts of relationships that we can be committed to but it is the romantic relationship that seems to draw all of the conversations we have when discussing relationships.

While we are looking and thinking about relationships, there are several thoughts that we need to mull over and come around to our own conclusions. The first thing that our society trains us to believe is that we have within all of us a need to find a lifelong wonderful sexual relationship that includes marriage and children. While the feudal lords of long ago needed marriage to establish paternity for inheritance purposes, the same rules no longer serve our society. Having raised two children as a single mother, I am here to tell you that having a partner who was present to share the load would have certainly been the preferred way of raising children, but it was not to be. Then again, if there had been a present partner who did not share parenting values, it would have resulted in added conflict. This, therefore, I have decided was the way my life was called to be. I drew to myself the lone parenting because I drew a partner that could not make a commitment. Since I was unable to commit, I was responsible for having been drawn to this partner by default. Friends can certainly attest to the fact we were "in love" at the time, but it was the love that was supposed to be for the time it was supposed to be and in the way it was supposed to be in order for both of our lives and the lives of those around us to evolve in the way they were to evolve for us all to experience what we were to experience.

When we give up the idea that we will have this forever relationship, we are free to enjoy the relationships we have while we have them. I recently heard from a family member that a marriage headed into its fortieth year was being dissolved because one partner had not been happy for a long time. If I were to use a societal judgment, as I tended to do, I did not understand why conversations could not have taken place over that forty years that would have kept this unhappiness at bay and allowed these two people to share the rest of their lives. This is not my domain, and it is not my situation, therefore, it is none of my business. This is the commitment situation that those two people and their families are being drawn into solving for the betterment of their evolution in this lifetime.

Some relationships are meant to last days, some for years, and whatever the relationship, they all last with us into eternity. Every relationship we enter into creates a thread that is woven into the tapestry of our lives and those lives are woven together eternally. We meet people and often have an instant bond. We feel as though we have known them our entire lives. This is because we have known them over and over and have lived enough lives together that we are beginning to recognize them when we meet in the current life. If you have had those kinds of people in your life, you will understand what I am talking about. If you have not, do not worry because it will happen to you at some time.

In order to work on the balances of our relationships we need to recognize that our sexual relationships are not necessarily our most intimate relationships. We often have close friends we confide in more than we do our sexual partner. If you have a partner that is also a confidante and a friend that you can trust no matter what happens, you have a keeper. An ideal relationship for me would be one where there is intimate interaction, unqualified caring, and yes, love, in the true sense, not necessarily the sexual sense. It would be a relationship that had survived several incarnations and was strong and firm and known to be so by both of us. We would accept each other and the lumps and bumps and flaws that come with that soul knowing that they would have you no other way than exactly how you are and you would change nothing about them either. We would be vibrationally and spiritually in tune.

We interact differently with everyone we encounter. Think of your friends and family members in general and you will see that everyone brings something different to your life and you contribute to their lives in a totally unique way. This is what we need to consider when we talk about the balance of love.

The second balancing activity (and this, like all others, is an ongoing activity) is one in which you begin writing down the names of those people with whom you interact. I would suggest writing a name when you see them or talk to them and not before. Once a name is on the list, put a tally mark next to it every time you see or talk to that person. Keep adding names and tally marks and keep track for at least two or three months. Don't get uptight or anal about it, there may be some days you just forget to pay attention. You will soon begin to see a pattern. Once you have seen the people that are a greater part of your days, you can take it to the next level. At that time you will look at what kind of a relationship you have. Is it a family relationship, a friendship, a lover, employer/employee, club connection, church or whatever? After you have established this, you can see if the balance is way off. Are the only connections you are having those of an employer/employee type? If so, you may want to add more friendship or church or family interactions. Sometimes family is far away, so we establish our friends and add a category of close friends/family. The categories don't matter, you will establish your own categories based on the relationships you encounter. I would not even have much of an employer/employee category since I am technically retired. Because I recently entered into a business partnership, however, this category has opened up a new list of friends and acquaintances that would be put into my repertoire. This is your list and your categorization, no one else's. Use it and let it help you balance your life as it involves loving relationships.

As you get better at this, you can also begin to take note of interactions that leave you feeling upset, angry, or sad, etc. Relationships that are not working for you need to be noted if you are going to successfully balance your life. At some point in time you will see that there are ongoing relationship problems that are keeping you from your own balance. Your best self can only operate on optimum efficiency if the love you give to others is reflected back to you. When you have relationships that are dragging you down, you owe it to your best self to absolve yourself of those relationships. This does not have to be done unkindly (because that would serve your best self no good either) but at some point in time it will need to be addressed and you will know when the time is right for you.

Some of us will have many categories that we ponder when we are balancing our relationships or the love we give to others. Some of us will not have very many at all or we may make larger groupings than others do. Once again, it does not matter how it is done, only that we use this as a tool to create a greater awareness of the relationships that do exist for us and what the frame of reference is for those relationships.

Remember too that each interaction provides a contact point. You may not have a lot of close friends but you may have many acquaintances. If you are a clerk (let's use Walmart as an example) you will have many interactions but those interactions will not in and of themselves be significant. What will be significant is that you have been given a venue in which to reach a broad number of people. The way in which you touch their lives may never be understood but it will have significance. **It is not in the number of interactions but in the quality of those interactions that we maintain our balance.** I find that I tend to think I am insignificant to others but when I do an exercise like this one, I understand that while I do not have a life partner at this time, I do interact with an amazing number of people over the course of a week and many of them are repeat interactions. When you begin to become aware of the nature, the duration, and the quality of your interactions and your relationships, you learn more about yourself, and this knowledge will lead you to striving more to be your best self. It is when you achieve this balance and are your best self for longer and longer periods of time that you contribute more fully to others achieving their connection with their best self.

In order to keep our balance when thinking of relationships, it is important that we try to see them as an observer. It is difficult to assess certain aspects of a relationship when we are a participant. I noticed this not long ago when I was describing a relationship where I did not want to give away exactly who I was discussing. As I explained it from a disassociated perspective, things about this relationship became much clearer and I began to see it from a different perspective than I previously had. Do not make judgments in either your own relationships or others that lead to added dysfunction and conflict. Women in particular tend to weave scenarios that are totally made up. We imagine stumbling blocks where there are none. We create our own worst scenario. In the fine art of balancing, we will begin releasing those kinds of thoughts and begin to retrain our minds to think differently.

INTROVERT/EXTROVERT, DOES IT MATTER?

There is a lot of information out there on introverts and extroverts in published material as well as internet information. For simplicity's sake we will think of an introvert as someone who is quiet and does not overtly approach others in a social setting. We often consider them to be shy individuals. We think of extroverts as being outgoing, enthusiastic individuals who are "life of the party" types. While these descriptions are not wrong, they are not exactly correct either.

The terms came into being in the early 20th century and were used by Carl Jung. These terms more accurately are endpoints on a spectrum that is much like a timeline. The introvert would be on the left end and the extrovert on the right end. There are graduating tendencies all along the way. If we establish the mid-point as being equal parts of introvert/extrovert then we can see that left of midpoint has more introvert or shy tendencies and right of mid- point is someone with more outgoing tendencies. There actually is a term used for this mid-point that probably comes closer to describing any of us and that is ambivert.

When we begin to balance different parts of our life, we naturally look at the social aspect of ourselves and how we interact with others. In studying the introvert/extrovert personalities, research is showing us that there is a genetic component that has much to do with which tendencies are strongest and there is much that can be attributed to the environment and how it influenced us. One very interesting thing that has come up in the research is that there is a difference not only in our social behavior but also in how we recharge our brains. Introverts tend to recharge by spending time alone. They lose energy when they are around people for long periods of time, especially crowds. Extroverts gain energy when around others. Being social charges them up. This knowledge could have a lot of significance for us. If we take someone who has introvert tendencies and have them involved in any group activity rather than a single activity, it would not provide the same balance as it would for a person with extrovert tendencies. Their brains react differently to stimuli and the entire pathway of the brain is affected differently. It will be up to you to study the introvert/extrovert tendencies you possess and assess yourself accordingly. Know that whatever you determine to be your overriding tendencies, you will need to take that into account in many different areas of your life.

There are several ways in which introverts need to be cared for in a positive way and this is good information for you to have whether you are an introvert or whether you have friends who are introverts (which means you all need to know this.).

1. Respect their need for privacy.
2. Never embarrass them in public
3. Let them observe first in new situations

4. Give them time to think, don't demand immediate answers.
5. Don't interrupt them.
6. Give them advance notice of expected changes in their life.
7. Give them fifteen minute warnings that time to finish tasks are at hand.
8. Reprimand them in private.
9. Teach them new skills privately
10. Enable them to find one best friend who has similar interests and abilities.
11. Don't push them to make lots of friends.
12. Respect their introversion and don't try to turn them into extroverts.

Just as the introvert has their tendencies to charging up privately, the extrovert has varying needs to be social. Because we either are, or have, extrovert tendencies or we know people who do, here are some caring tips that will help us be better friends and more thoroughly tend to leading us on a path to our best selves.

1. Respect their independence
2. Compliment them in the company of others.
3. Accept and encourage their enthusiasm.
4. Allow them to explore and talk things out.
5. Thoughtfully surprise them.
6. Understand when they are busy.
7. Let them dive right in.

8. Offer them options.
9. Make physical and verbal gestures of affection.
10. Let them shine.

Just as we have mentioned, the classification of the ambivert probably more accurately describes most of us with leaning a bit to the left or a bit to the right. While they do not experience the great differences between the two, they are a more balanced personality.

The need for this information is to become aware. We become aware of our differences and our similarities. We understand that because we have a difference in the way we approach life and situations, we react differently also. When we realize that these differences can enhance our lives if we deal with them adequately, then we are stepping closer to meeting the needs we have in our quest for balancing our best self.

{The lists of ways to care for both the introvert and extrovert was from a shared graphic on Facebook- original source unknown}

GENEROSITY VS. GENEROUS SPIRIT

We use all sorts of terms when we describe our friends to someone. One of these terms usually has to do with their generosity. When we think of the word generosity, we usually think in terms of how freely a person gives money to causes. That is one kind of generosity. We also have generosity of our time, and that is a much rarer commodity. Many people would much rather write a check than donate their time. Others are generous with their family but not so generous with others. I have a friend whose husband was very generous at Christmas time, but at other times in the year, he kept a tight rein on the household expenses. When their children and grandchildren would come to the house and order pizzas, they would all chip in rather than having "dad" foot the bill. Now, there is absolutely nothing wrong with this approach but it showcases the degree of generosity this man possessed. He showed generosity at some times and not at other times, as many of us do. When we want to be generous with our time, we find the time. When we don't want to be generous with our time, we are "too busy." Same with our generosity with money. While we may have money to donate to the church of our choice, we may find it difficult to donate to the local food pantry. We use the excuse that if people would only get out and get a job, they would have money for food. We have situational generosity much of the time. We see people near a busy intersections with a sign asking for money and we don't give them any because we figure they would just go to the local liquor store instead of the local grocery store. We make a judgment based on no information whatsoever rather than part with a five-dollar bill. We are using our situational generosity to justify our lack of generosity.

Another kind of generosity is generosity of spirit. I like this kind of generosity, and it is the kind I strive for. It is the kind of generosity that strikes us in the initial moment. When you see someone with a sign asking for money, if your first instinct is to reach in and pull out a five-dollar bill and give to them, then that is what you should do. That is an example of a generous spirit. A generous- spirited person will follow- up on a generous thought and not be swayed by any other thought. There will no longer be any thoughts of, "Well, I ought to," or "Well, I should." When you think that a cause sounds worthy, you will find a way to get involved. We get many solicitations for money from various places all year. We can donate a minimal amount to each cause or we can decide which causes to can support with a larger donation. The matter of a cash donation is really not the point, it just is an example of the different ways we can be generous. I choose to support two or three major causes each year and save a portion of my donations for causes that may pop up unexpectedly.

Some of the most generous people I know do not give money, but they give their time. Time is valuable. There are often physical, skill, and location limitations involved when we consider donating our time. It may be that we have a devotion to a cause but because of some factor out of our control, we can only support that cause through a cash donation. Once again, it really doesn't matter how we give or what we give. **If we are hoping to have a balanced life, it is only important that we find a way to give.**

When we are balanced, we will understand the difference between generosity and a generous spirit and we will become a generous- spirited person as a result of our balance. Generosity of spirit is one of the most valuable traits a person in balance can possess. We have all been given certain talents, abilities, and blessings. When we share those with others, we expand who we are. We become more than we are like a rosebud as it blooms. The rosebud is gorgeous, but as each day passes, that bud loosens and loosens and begins to unfold into its full beauty. Generosity does that to us. We, like the rose, are beautiful in all stages, but the whole point of the rose bush is to show fully formed roses. We enjoy every stage of the rose, but the point is for the flower to become its fullest version of itself. So it is with us. We are beautiful regardless of where we are in our development. When we are blessed with a generous spirit, we grow and blossom into the beauty for which we were intended.

Think about your own generosity. Think about and list organizations that get your money and organizations that get your time. Think also about the things you do for friends and family. While baking cookies for your neighbor's birthday would not fall under charitable contributions in the eyes of the IRS, it would be an indication of a generous spirit and should be listed.

Time with family is a bit trickier. We love our family and want to spend time with them but sometimes we over extend ourselves with our family because we do have a generous spirit. It is very easy for family to take a generous -spirited person for granted. What was once generously given then becomes a chore and something to be dreaded. I found myself in this situation, and I am still working on achieving a balance that I can live with and enjoy without resentment. Anytime you go from enjoying the giving you are doing to resenting the giving you are doing, you need to reassess the balance involved. Generosity of spirit has no room for resentment. If that happens, it morphs into something that is not remotely related to generosity of any kind. Getting the balance is the key.

You can be a very generous-spirited person and still say "no" when the situation warrants. You do not have to feel any obligation to keep giving. Generosity in its basest definition is something that is given freely. If you are shamed or coerced into giving, that is not giving, that is manipulation. That is not remotely involved in generosity, but many groups and individuals play upon emotions to get a person to give something to them. Probably all of us have been a victim of this kind of operation at some time and that is why, perhaps, we have become leery about opportunities requesting our time or money. I think of the times I have spent involved in church activities. The more I did the more I was asked to do. I noted the same thing in other groups I was involved in. All of a sudden, because I didn't want to upset anyone, I found myself over extended and too busy to find time for myself. I did not know how to delicately withdraw so I chose to totally withdraw from the organizations themselves. Total withdrawal is not the most balanced approach, but it was what I did at the time. I am considering re-aligning myself with a couple of these organizations. When I do it will be with a much different mindset, and I will not second-guess myself when I decline a volunteer job. You can have a generous spirit without being a doormat. That is always good to remember.

Thus far I have discussed the major categories of generosity which involve time and money. There are some activities that indicate a generous spirit which involve neither time nor money and are often overlooked. When you smile at someone you don't know, you are exhibiting a generous spirit. When you pick something up off of the floor in a department store and put it back on the shelf, you are exhibiting a generous spirit. Any time you do something with no thought of any kind of reparation, you are exhibiting a generous spirit. I think of one thing that we don't consider: doing what is expected even when it isn't required. When we are at a restaurant that has litter bins and it is understood that we will bus our own tables, it is a generous spirited person who observes that tradition. I see time and time again where people just get up and leave their dishes for others to clean up. Doing what is expected of you even when others don't indicates a generous spirit. You do not need the "clean-up police" to stand over you, you are generous enough to clean up after yourself. When we observe traffic laws we are exhibiting our generosity, we are thinking of the safety of others as well as our own.

Are you a much more generous spirited person than you thought? It is the intent to do for others that shows the degree of generosity. Not everyone is blessed and gifted in the same way, and their form of generosity will not be the same as yours. The form that your generosity takes does not matter, it only matters that you give as you are called from within to give. You will blossom when you do, and you will be gaining the balance that will help you achieve your best self.

I spent a great deal of my life in a state that was void of much generosity. I found excuses to avoid giving of my resources to others, and I never had the time to devote to a good cause. I had brief periods of time where some cause or other caught my eye and I opened myself to being generous. I did enjoy the experience, but I did not connect it with leading to a better self. I did not fully understand what having a generous spirit can do for you. I was raised in an environment where we took care of ourselves, did not ask others for help, and expected others to take care of themselves. If a neighbor was in need, we would help, otherwise it was no one's business. I clearly remember when I was applying for scholarships to college. When my dad realized he would have to fill out all sorts of information about his financial business he told me to just forget it because he was not going to fill them out. It was none of anyone's business other than the IRS what was going on financially in the Zimmerman household. We did not get to send invitations to high school graduation out because that would be like "asking for gifts." I share this not to point out that this in any way is "wrong," but rather to point out that this is my frame of reference for generosity to others.

I had to learn to be generous. I came to acknowledge that the feeling that was created within me was magnified when it was generously shared with others. It was a very sporadic education. I would find myself being generous, then tight-fisted. I would be afraid that if I gave away too much I would not have enough left for me and what I wanted. I had not yet understood the flow of abundance that is in the Universe and how it works. This flow of abundance is a byproduct of our generosity and we will discuss it as it intertwines and works as we strive to be our best self. The enhancement of a generous spirit serves us all in proportion to our devotion to that spirit. Generosity cannot be faked if we are to be our best self. We must truly enjoy the giving process and its results more than we enjoy the complacency of a non-generous lifestyle.

KINDNESS AND COMPASSION

As my children grew up, I always tried to teach them to be kind. I would tell them that kindness doesn't cost anything and it was very important that they always tried to be kind. I am not sure that I set the best example, but I tried. I found it easier to be kind than I did to be patient. I would lose my patience and as a result kindness often flew out of the window right along with patience. But I tried. My kids have both grown to be very kind individuals and I hope they are passing this information on to my grandchildren. I will repeat it for all of you – **kindness doesn't cost a thing and it can mean the world to someone else.**

Kindness is much like generosity in that it is a gift to someone. When we treat anyone kindly, we are sharing a bit of our spirit with their spirit. I have some former students on my Facebook page, and I am surprised every once in awhile when they reach out and share their feelings about me as a teacher. I had one such discussion yesterday with a person whose posts I like; the posts are funny, quirky, and usually have a tinge of sarcasm. She was a lot like this in the 6th grade. I remember that she was respectful but always on the edge of disrespect. She never tipped over the edge, but I think it would have been easy for her to do so. She reflected on the time she spent in my class favorably and I was honored. I was a tough teacher. I expected good behavior and I expected students to do the work I asked them to do. I saw potential when they didn't, and I tried in the only way I knew how to get the best out of them. I didn't always succeed, but as adults every one of them seem to understand now what they didn't understand then: that I cared.

I taught school for years and believe me, it was difficult to be kind at times. The American teacher is expected to perform miracles with each and every mind that enters the classroom, whether the student wants to learn or not. I worked with fifth graders (10/11 year olds) for sixteen years and sixth graders (11/12 year olds) for another seventeen years. During this time I was also raising a boy and a girl of my own. I had kids 24/7. This was a drain. There were many times, I was not kind to anyone, myself included.

My mother was also a teacher. She taught until she became pregnant with me and then took time off to stay at home with me and my sister. When I was in the fourth grade, the year before my sister started school, she had a chance to get back into the classroom as a second grade teacher. She took that opportunity. She had gained a two- year degree when she started teaching and had a life license that meant she did not have to get her bachelor's degree to continue to teach. She chose to use her summers to go back to school and get her bachelor's degree in education any way. She was in her early forties at the time. She was definitely pulled in all directions and could easily lose her patience and did on a regular basis. The problem ,as I saw it, was that she was a very kind and patient teacher yet a very impatient and demanding parent. I told her one time when I was in junior high that I didn't think it was fair that she used all of her patience on other kids and didn't have any left over for her own kids. I don't know whether I thought that bit of information would make a difference, but I felt compelled to share it with her and I remember it to this day. Perhaps her lack of patience was somehow related to my need to share my not so kind thoughts with her.

I learned patience (what I have of it, anyway) and kindness when I had children myself. I wanted to be different for them than my parents had been for me when it came to a loving home. I wanted to hug my kids and I wanted to be soft with them, not sharp. I did not have parents who mistreated me, but I did not have parents who were particularly aware of some of my emotional needs. In all fairness, their parenting was cultural. I am not sure that parents in the fifties – any of them- took their kid's emotional needs into consideration. I believe that those of us who became parents in the nineteen seventies did so with different parenting ideas because of the parenting we had as children. Life evolves generationally. Our children and grandchildren will parent differently than we did. This is not a condemnation nor is it a judgment, it is merely an observation. As you consider your own kindness and patience, consider this difference.

When we discuss kindness, we can take kindness one step further to compassion. Compassion is to kindness much as a generous spirit is to generosity; it is the next step up. When we are kind, it is usually a single effort. Compassion encompasses much more than mere kindness. Compassion becomes the essence of how we relate to everyone we meet. We look at someone, anyone, and find ourselves hoping they have a fulfilling life. We hope they are well and that they are fed and housed. We become concerned that all is right in their world. We hear about people we don't know having troubles, and we find ourselves sending out a thought of kindness that they will be able to have the strength and help available to overcome this trouble. This is compassion. Compassion is our soul expressing kindness. When we have compassion we cannot react any way but with kindness. We may have a grinchy-snarky thought once in a while after all we are still human, but it is only a passing remnant of our former self.

When we are working on balancing our best self, we can work on the kindness we show others very incrementally. We can begin by simply noticing all of the times that we have unkind thoughts. Does this happen often? Are those thoughts random, or are they directed at specific individuals? How often do we react kindly to others? Are there some interactions that are easier for us to react to kindly? What are they? After you have evaluated the trend of your thoughts, you can progress to another exercise. When you have an unkind thought, you can begin to dismiss it and replace it with a kind thought. Just having an awareness of your thoughts and emotions will be the step you need to take to get this into balance. As you react more kindly to others, you will see that there is a different reaction others have to you. Others reflect back to you what you are giving to them, much like a mirror. You will begin to notice the kindness of others.

Studies have been done that have shown that when random acts of kindness are performed, the giver and the receiver both experience a higher amount of the feel-good hormones dopamine and serotonin. The study also revealed that anyone who observes an act of kindness also has an increased amount of these hormones. Kindness makes a difference emotionally and physiologically. Kindness, like generosity, does not have to be massive to make a difference in your life or in the life of someone else. It just has to be authentically expressed and performed. In order for it to be the best balance for you, it needs to become as natural as breathing. One very easy expression of a kind act is simply the prolific use of "please," "thank you," and "excuse me." These phrases are ones that we teach our children but often forget to use ourselves. There is a current expression, "my bad," which I believe means, "excuse me, I am at fault." I personally do not use it, but I recognize it as being used in the way it is intended. Any time we do not take over a situation and allow someone else the courtesy of having the reins, we are acting kindly. You reach a line together and let the other person go first, that is being kind. A kind smile instead of a sneer when a child is acting up, is kind, and I am sure is appreciated by a frazzled parent. There are numerous ways that we can treat others kindly' and, as I told my children many years ago, "it costs you nothing."

HOW DO I LOOK?

Sometimes we experience a life that is out of balance because we become so consumed with the perception of how we look. We listen to the ego. Our concern may not be how we appear physically as far as size and beauty, but how we appear socially. Do we have a car that looks okay to everyone else? Is our house an embarrassment? As we age, we question our wrinkles, our hair color, and our aging stride. We even, at times in our life, are questioning how our partner or our children are perceived by our friends. My parents loved my son and daughter so much, but I remember a time when Andrew was at the mall with my mother. When they got back, she told me that she was almost embarrassed to be seen with Andrew because he had long hair. I could not believe she would even feel this way, yet, I had to admit that I often questioned how my friends perceived my long-haired son. At that time long hair on guys was not a typical style and males who chose to wear their hair longer were judged similar to those who have piercings and tattoos. The same thing can be said when women wear their hair short; guys like the long hair and view a short-haired female as not being as feminine. Writing this down and reading it makes me realize that society can have some pretty screwy ideas at times, but, what is even more unnerving, is that we buy into that idiocy.

As we age, what we find acceptable in our life changes. What needs to be understood, if we are to exist as our best self, is that it truly does not matter. We are going to change. Because of all the facts of life, **change is the only constant.** Nothing ever stays the same. We take each day as it is given to us. We know ourselves for that bit of time only. If we are given another day, we will take that day as it is. And so it goes, day after day. To look back and bemoan anything that happened does us no good because that time is gone, over, and never to be repeated. To spend time thinking of the future is also a study in the absurd because we will never get there. When we reach a "future" time, it will become our now. **There is only now. That is all there ever is.**

You look how you look now. You are how you are now. The weather is what it is now. Everything is happening now. There is no past and there is no future, it is all now. This is one of the most mind-expanding ideas we can embrace. We have been taught about the past and the future. We have had the past thrown in our faces as a way to keep us in a state of guilt. We have future continuously waved in front of us causing us to totally ignore now. We miss out on the excitement of our now because we are focusing on some mythical tomorrow. This is destination addiction at its best, or I should say, at its worst. This idea that whatever is ahead of us is better than what we have now keeps us from enjoying the present moment. Think back on "the good old days" in your life. Did you realize that you were living the good old days when it was in your now? Probably not. I think of the song "those were the days, my friend, we thought they'd never end" but they did, and hopefully we were not so focused on the future that we didn't enjoy them. The good news is, it is never too late. You can begin today and focus on today to make it the best day of your life. That is the kind of balance we hope for in this part of our journey.

Several years ago, my moods were often guided by the weather. I was never diagnosed with Seasonal Affective Disorder, but I was definitely able to function better on a sunny day than I was on a dreary day. One of the balances I have been able to successfully embrace is that of no longer letting the weather affect my mood. I look at every day and accept that for today, the weather is perfect. It sounds goofy, perhaps, but if you try it, you will see that when you change the way you think about the weather for just this one day, you will no longer allow it to distract you from your enjoyment of life.

One of the keys to balancing your best self is looking at everything for today and now only. How you look, how you feel, and how your react are all available only now. **When you change how you look at things, those very things you are looking at change and become balanced.** In the process, you become balanced and you experience life in the best possible way, in the now.

As I think about balance in my life, I consider several things. While I believe that I am an attractive, relatively young-looking sixtyish woman, I have to admit a few things about that. One of the most difficult is that I am no longer in my thirties! I will never see thirty again and when I compare my body, my hair, my skin texture and skin tone, and my level of physical energy to that time in my life, I will certainly come up lacking. It is when I look at myself with a fresh eye as a mid- sixtyish and assess myself more realistically that I can find more self-acceptance. This, after all, is the most important goal that any of us need when we are balancing our life. We need to have a secure self-acceptance of ourselves and our abilities. We would not attempt to compare a toddler with a teenager when it comes to certain criteria, so why would we try to evaluate someone based on a thirty- plus year age difference. It would be like comparing apples to oranges, it cannot be fairly done, yet that is what we do, constantly. We compare ourselves to someone younger, thinner, taller, wealthier, etc. The standard doesn't matter. Our ego continuously attempts to convince us that we are somehow inept in some way. **A life of balance will require us to set our own standards sans the ego.**

DON'T BE A WHINEY-ASS

One of the easiest ways to throw ourselves out of balance is to become whiney about what we encounter in life. Regardless of where we are in life and what is going on in our life, we have drawn it to ourselves. Yes, either by our conscious or our unconscious efforts, we have become what we are because of our thoughts about many different things from the time we were able to discern our thoughts. We were just unaware that was what we were doing.

There are some universal truths that apply to everyone. Gravity is an example. It is not a matter of whether you live in the United States or Norway, you are affected by gravity in the same way. We understand gravity. There are other laws that are always in operation. One of these is known as the Law of Attraction. It is just as real as gravity but is not as well understood. The Law of Attraction basically says that which is like is drawn to itself. It is a frequency vibration that attracts like vibrations. There was a movie, "The Secret," that brought this law to public awareness. **The Law of Attraction is always at work, drawing to us that which we are thinking about and focusing our attention on.**

As physicists tell us, everything is energy. When we are able to focus our vibration in a way that will match the vibration of what we are wanting in our life, we will have what we want. This matching is what we have done, but it has usually been accidentally without our ever realizing that was what we did. When we focused on getting an education, we achieved it. When we have focused on being employed, we achieved it. Any time we zeroed in on a desire and maintained an unwavering focus on that desire, we achieved it. We gave up the control of how it would happen or when it would happen, and we just focused on the achievement. This is how the Law of Attraction works, so we might as well have it work for us rather than against us.

This is why it does not pay to be a whiney-ass. When we whine, we focus on what we do not want. If we are focusing on what we do not want, we will attract more of what we do not want. A practiced focus is necessary if we are to become deliberate creators of our lives. As we think of balancing our lives, we often just whine about what we don't have. The more we whine, the more miserable we become. In order to get the balance back, we have to decide a few things. We need to take time, whatever time we need, and decide exactly what it is that we do want. How do we picture our life? If there were no barriers whatsoever, how would a day in our life play out? How would we look, how would we walk, how would we laugh, and how would we spend our time? Who would our friends be? What kind of activities would we take part in? What would we cook, or would we even cook? Would we live where we live? Think our lives through thoroughly and often. After much of this mind work, we will come to a conclusion about what we want for our life.

There may be many things we think about and as we think about them, we don't think we could achieve them. If you do not believe in your imagination that you are capable of achieving the goal, then you won't. I could think about being an Olympic gold medalist as a pole-vaulter, but as a sixtyish woman who has never been athletic in any way, it is not something I think I could ever be capable of, therefore, it is not a valid projection nor will it be anywhere near a vibrational match to be drawn to me. I can, however, picture me working in my garden with energy and enjoyment, cooking healthy foods on my grill with friends nearby, and traveling to enjoyable destinations. I can also see myself as a successful author with a loyal following. Because I can see my life in this way, it is achievable. When I am able to maintain my focus, I can achieve it.

One very important aspect of envisioning what we want must be stressed. It is when you focus on the completion of the desire, the actualization of the desire, and the knowledge that it is already coming to you that you will gain it. Using the travel aspect of my vision, I cannot be consumed with worry about how I will ever afford the travel I want, or when I will find the time, who I would travel with, etc. This is the place where we begin to question the whens and hows and this is where we go all whiney and why we think that the Law of Attraction is not working. It is at this point where the vibrations begin to shift back and forth and we lose the achievement of having our desire. It may shift our point of attraction to such a degree that we never realize our dreams, and then we think we are unlucky or undeserving. Nothing could be further from the truth. Any time we have a desire and know that it will come to us, we will achieve it. This does not mean that we will achieve the exact desire, but we will achieve the essence of our desire. I am looking forward to the day where I gain millions of dollars from a lottery win. The essence of my desire is enough wealth that I no longer have to be concerned about money in my life. I can get the essence of my desire without having a lottery win.

Whining about what we are lacking only creates more lack. The more we whine, the more we have to whine about. If we are going to create a balance in our lives, we have to learn how to give up the whining. The easiest way sounds a bit too easy, but it is to simply be thankful for what we have in life. Let what we have serve to be enough. Once again, it is not always easy to be thankful if we have less than what we think we should have, but it is the only way we can change our vibration sufficiently enough to change our point of attraction. And, be very clear on this point, we cannot simply pretend to be okay with what we have if we are not truly okay with what we have. We have to genuinely find a way to transmute our thinking. We have to look at what we have and find way to make that enough in our life for now. When we live strictly in the now, we lose the anxiety that is created by concern for the future.

We can take tremendous lessons from nature when we think about how humans give in to whining and how to twist our way totally out of that mode. I have squirrels in my backyard that I dearly love to watch. They run up and down and around the oak and walnut trees with great abandon. Not once do you see them stop and try to figure out where they are going to get their next meal or where they are going to sleep at night. They just concentrate on doing what squirrels do, which is be a squirrel. They do not think they are not as good as the birds and spend time wishing they were birds. They just enjoy their lives right now. They do not have watches they refer to so that they can plan the next hour, they just are. This is why the natural world thrives the way it does. This existence does not mean that there may not be a hawk lying in wait for one of these squirrels, but the threat of a hawk does not deter their enjoyment of the now. We look at the "hawks" of our life and worry and stew over them, and it keeps us from thoroughly enjoying our now. We whine over the "hawks."

Daffodils do not whine because they are not roses. Daffodils stand proud and tall and shine brightly in the early spring. They do not worry if their stems are too large. They just present their beauty for our enjoyment. The beautiful dandelion does not whine because many people call it a weed. The dandelion knows it is one of the most beneficial plants on the earth and as such stands proud and provides early nectar for the bees. It does not suffer from a poor self-image. The grand and glorious milkweed that is being systematically removed from farm ground is necessary for the life of the Monarch butterfly larvae. Its destruction is a product of human ego and nothing more. This destruction is the product of a whiney farmer who cannot appreciate it for the beneficial plant that it is. When we get human ego involved in the whiney process, nature suffers until we make a choice to stop it. As we become aware of how the whininess in our lives affects everything around us, we will continue to whine. Once we realize the futility of whining, we will look for alternative ways to deal with our moments of now, and it will have a ripple effect that will be passed on and on.

To get a handle on how much whining you are doing and to understand how it is throwing you off balance, you need to turn to your journal. As you begin to recognize whiney thoughts, write them down. Once you acknowledge a whiney thought you are made aware of it. If it repeats itself, you can, because you are now aware of it, simply cast it aside and no longer dwell on it. Awareness is the first way in which we can effectively deal with our whiney vibrations and often awareness is all that is needed. You are now aware and you easily release the recurring thoughts. Sometimes more is needed. You may look at the whiney thoughts and with some you may feel justified by having that thought....."Yes, but I know I am right, blah, blah, blah." This kind of approach just draws out the whininess. We are using our ego to keep us off balance. The ego does this because as long as we are off balance our ego is remaining in charge and important. It is at this point that we need to ask ourselves if we want to regain balance, or do we want to pander to an approach that isn't serving us. You have to decide. No one can make these decisions for you.

I am in the middle of one of those perfect illustrations of an ego-endorsed irritation. It is one that I find puzzling because a greater part of me does not have any concern about the outcome. This involves a family member that I am not close to. There have been certain choices made by this family member that have directly affected others in her close family. She has always been rather self-absorbed but I have never thought of her as unkind. She has made some decisions that have caused deep grief to those who have loved her for years. This is not a situation that I am close to either physically or emotionally. Why, then, am I making it a problem for me to deal with? To regain my balance, I first realize that it is not my problem. I then have to take a good hard look at what my motivation is for keeping this in my vibration. When I do this, it is a realization that does not bode well. My ego is using this as a way for me to feel superior to this relative. This was a woman who held herself a bit above others (me included) when relationship difficulties presented themselves. She has cast herself as superior many times over many people. Now that she is the one kicking a forty year marriage to the curb, she seems to think nothing of the hurt she is causing. Now I am wanting to feel the superiority. That is what we have to deal with when we work on keeping our balance. We are very often called upon to see things about ourselves that are often not pleasant. The great news is that once these glitches are brought to the light of our awareness, we can deal with them. We can understand our motivation and we can kick it to the curb. This is not the time to castigate ourselves. We simply acknowledge how we feel and send those feelings on their way. This does not mean that we will not have these thoughts pass again, but we can now say, "Oh, there it is again, bye bye."

As we study our whining patterns, we begin to become aware of negative vibrations sooner and more easily. We accept the need to pass them on and we get yet another step closer to balancing our lives.

COMPARING OURSELVES TO????????

Through the years, I have figured out quite a bit about comparing ourselves to others because I have spent an inordinate amount of time comparing myself to everyone I encounter. I have not always compared clearly and with any kind of a motive, but I realized this quite innocently when I was meeting with the Chicks of "66," which is a group of women I went to high school with. They started meeting bi-monthly for lunch and any ladies from the class are invited to attend if they are in the area. We have a group of grads that are on Facebook, and we have reconnected in the last few years. I have only been able to meet with this group once, but it was fun and rather enlightening. I looked at these faces and most looked, to me, like they had aged very well. There were some who had aged well, but they didn't look like I remember them looking. One in particular I remember thinking was "cute" in high school. I guess there are not many mid-60 ladies who can be called "cute," but it was another example of times that I realize that I tend to categorize people.

It took a long time for me to realize that many times the very act of categorization can cause an imbalance in vibrational alignment. I can sit here at Panera, writing, and observing. If I observe those who come in and decide, perhaps because I have certain concerns on my mind, that they fit in a category. If I am stressing over my finances, for example, I may categorize people I have never seen and may never see again as either having more or less than I do. I don't do this to feel inferior or superior, I do it unconsciously because it is, for some reason, helping keep me grounded. Or so I convince myself. What I am doing is keeping myself out of balance because I am reinforcing my worry about my finances. When we categorize and compare ourselves to anyone else for any reason, we are projecting on to others the insecurities we are feeling. The more we project, the more we keep ourselves vibrating in a lesser vibration that will keep the very thing we are desiring away from us. When we categorize others, we are making an unfair comparison. It is not doing our interaction with them any good, nor is it doing us any good.

Categorizing is simply one kind of comparison we make. There are others. Other comparisons are even less productive and more dangerous. We may make a comparison that becomes a judgment. That judgment then morphs into a negative assessment of our life. It can keep us off balance for an indeterminate amount of time with very undesirable results. We compare and our ego will convince us that we are the ones that come up short on the comparison meter. One thing about these kinds of comparisons that is very interesting is that we never compare ourselves in areas where we are confident. We only compare when we are having self-doubt. We only compare and judge when we are looking at a situation in which we feel inferior and we are wanting to find a way to twist our thinking so that we can be put on a superior plane. When we know, for example, that we look nice, we do not look at others with an eye to put them down. We have no reason to. When we are not sure that what we are wearing looks good on us, we will look at other with a much more critical eye, trying to convince ourselves that we look "better than that lady."

There was a rather interesting study done years ago that I have always remembered. A group of women were given a set of women's silhouettes. The women were instructed to choose the silhouette that most closely matched their body. In over 90% of the cases, women consistently chose silhouettes that were larger than they actually were. When men were given male silhouettes and given the same instructions, they consistently chose images that were smaller or more well- built than they were. Females and males have been so thoroughly indoctrinated by society that body images are not realistic for either of the sexes. When we expect to find balance by comparisons, we will continue to remain off balance.

Comparisons are not an evil aberration. They are often a result of observation only. We can look at someone and think about their hairstyle if we are considering a change of hair style. We may compare the sizes of small children if we are wondering if a child is older or younger than our own grandchild. Comparisons are often simply observations and nothing more. It is when we use these comparative observations to make a self-judgment that they will keep us off balance. If I look at every female I encounter trying to decide if I am larger or smaller or look better or worse than they do, I will remain unbalanced. I did this for years and I understand from personal experience how much this kind of behavior can keep you from being in balance with your best self. I still have to fight this tendency if I am experiencing negative emotions and feelings.

The only time a comparison can help you regain a balance is when you compare you to yourself. When you look at the "you" of today and compare it to the "you" of yesterday and can see that you are living life closer to being in balance, you are using a comparison in a helpful way. We may try to convince ourselves that we are only comparing so we can make decisions about what we want for ourselves, but that is delusional. We are judging that what we already are is not good enough and that we need to change. **The truth is that we do not need to compare ourselves to anyone else for any reason, we are already good enough.** We have listened to our ego long enough and we have believed it often enough that we think we need to make the comparisons, but we don't.

Balance will be steps closer when we truly realize that we no longer need to compare ourselves to any others for any reason.

SOLITUDE VS LONELINESS

Many people become overly concerned about relationships. I have those concerns too. I consider relationships that are working or not working with family members. I consider a lack of intimate romantic relationships. I think of friendship that exist now and those that have faded over the years. There are different ways we can consider any relationship. We can contemplate it as is now, as it was at a previous time, as we wish it were now, or as we wish it had been. Now, if we look at our relationship questions from a place of balance, we will look at them much differently. The first thing we will realize is that viewing them from a previous time and place is a dead end. They were what they were and existed for the time they were to have been there, either for us or for the other person. Because all is forever, yet fleeting, we never truly lose a relationship, it simply changes in time, place, and form. Nothing physical lasts forever. Matter has a shelf life. It is only the essence and the energy of essence that is eternal.

When we accept that what we attach ourselves to physically has a beginning and an ending, it allows us to consider relationships much differently. We become able to more freely enjoy the relationships we are given at any time. We can look at a friendship and enjoy it for today, for now, knowing that for whatever reason, it will be temporal. This holds true in romantic relationships.

Let us say, we meet the love of our life at age twenty-five. We marry, we have a family, and we grow into old age together. At some point in time, there will be a physical parting of the ways. It is inevitable, and for us to believe otherwise is beyond crazy. Sometimes that ending is with a break up and sometimes it is with a death, but there is an eventual parting of the physical.

When we talk about balance, we realize something wonderful. While there is a physical divide, there is not an energetic divide. The energy is still there, it is not lost...... ever!

This knowledge can help us deal with life on a daily basis if we will let it. When we are without a partner and perhaps living away from family and friends, we sometimes give way to feelings of loneliness. Loneliness is much different from the feeling we get when we are alone and enjoying fixing a meal of our choice or alone and reading a good book. Loneliness is the kind of alone feeling that comes from a sense of lack rather than a sense of freedom. When we do not attach ourselves to others, we are more freely able to pass our time alone with enjoyment, rather than need. It is not always easy, because we have watched romantic movies and read romantic novels and have come to believe that love exists in only one form, the romantic sexual love. When we view love in this way, it creates its own neediness that is a very inaccurate representation of love.

There is an art to being alone on a continual basis. We have to learn to enjoy our own company. When I was first divorced, even though I had two small children, I was constantly looking for avenues that would allow me to escape being home at dusk. That was a difficult time for me to be alone at home, even though I wasn't really alone because my kids were there. Thirty plus years later, that time of day sometimes magnifies my solitude. It is a time where any distraction is welcomed. It is not a conscious dread, but it is often just an unsettled feeling that ebbs once I acknowledge it. I am a very social creature by nature even though there have been many times that I have chosen to withdraw from people and live a hermit-like existence. I enjoy interaction and that is probably why I enjoy social media as much as I do. It is not the technology I enjoy, but the connection with other sentient beings who share common interests.

Loneliness is much different than aloneness. Loneliness has an emptiness component to it that aloneness does not. Aloneness exists when you are leading a solitary life and are actually by yourself for the major part of your time. Loneliness can occur when you are in a room full of people. Some of the loneliest times in my life were felt when I was in a floundering marriage. When we have expectations that there will be emotional or social support from someone outside ourselves, and we don't get that support, we experience that sad kind of loneliness that results from unresolved expectations.

If we are going to lead a balanced life, we need to look at our times of aloneness fairly and bravely. How much time do we spend alone? Is this amount of time causing us a problem, or are we okay with it? If we have little alone time, do we need more? Are we allowing for not only time alone but also unencumbered time where we can indulge in activities of our own choosing? Do we ever feel lonely? Is there a certain time of the day or year when this occurs? (Often holiday times exacerbate feelings of loneliness.) Are feelings of loneliness fleeting or do they consume blocks of time that keep us from enjoying our life?

Sociological studies have shown that people who maintain a good social life age in a much healthier way. To be alone too much can be detrimental to our health. It is much easier to resolve being alone than it is to resolve loneliness. If there is a secret to avoiding loneliness, it may indirectly involve our thoughts. For example, although I am alone most of the time, I seldom experience loneliness. If I were to dwell on my time alone, I could easily convince myself that I am lonely, and that is often what happens to some. Many people use these words interchangeably and feel like they are lonely when they are just actually experiencing solitude.

It is here where I must, in all fairness, issue a disclaimer. Although I lead a solitary life and I am alone for probably 60% of my time, I will find somewhere to go most days in order to socialize. Even if it is just to go shopping I will get out of the house in order to be around other people.

If you are balancing your life, you will make certain that you do not have neither too little nor too much solitude. You will look to interaction with family and friends to provide you with the connections you need to keep yourself vibrationally tuned up. The easiest way to avoid loneliness is to look for ways to help others. When you get out of your sad place to a kind and compassionate place, the loneliness will ebb and a balance will result. Each of us responds to our aloneness in a way that is unique to us, and each of us will need to find that balance in a way that is unique. For some, it will not be a matter of too much time alone, but not enough time alone. Every path will be different, but the key to making it work is to balance time alone and time with others.

YOU ARE WHAT YOU EAT

We hear time and time again that we are what we eat. This is true because our cells are constantly replenishing themselves. The body we have today has none of the same cells that it had a mere seven years ago. Our blood cells, our skin cells, and all the cells in our body are dying and are being replaced as you are reading this. If we are feeding our bodies food that contains toxic substances what results will not be as healthy as it will be if we are feeding it healthy, non-toxic foods. This chapter is not about weight loss. This chapter is going to give you some ideas that can help you keep your body physically in balance as it pertains to what you ingest.

The first thing to consider when keeping our bodies in balance is that we have to realize these physical bodies are about 80% water. If we are to honor these bodies that house the non-physical part of us, then it is important that they stay hydrated. As much as I enjoy a good cup of coffee, water is what will keep us hydrated, not coffee, or tea, or any other liquid drinks. There are many theories about how much water we need. As I grew up, my health classes taught that we should have about eight 8 oz. glasses of water per day, or about 64 oz. (2 quarts). Now, I read articles that say we should drink half of our weight in water per day. Some suggest 100 oz. per day.

I do not believe there is a one size fits all answer for how much water we need to drink. If we want to work on a balance, we need to be aware of how much water we are drinking. To figure this out, we cannot take into consideration coffee, tea, soft drinks, etc. We need to keep track of how much actual water we drink for a period of one or two weeks. Is it a consistent amount daily? The base amount appears to be 64 oz. If we drink a significant amount that is less than that, our electrolytes can get out of balance and that will throw different bodily functions off and our body will not work as efficiently as it should.

If we are not drinking enough water, our body will hold on to the water we drink in an effort to maintain its equilibrium. Our kidneys will not function as often and because they serve as a filter to get rid of toxins in the body, we are not going to be ridding the body of those toxins as easily. If we drink too much water our kidneys become over taxed in their elimination of toxins as well as potassium and magnesium and other minerals our body needs for optimal functioning. The key to keeping our bodies working at maximum efficiency starts with getting enough water in our system. When we do that, the body's natural filtration system will cooperate as it is meant to.

Another reminder also pertains to keeping our body systems in good working order has to do with roughage. It isn't discussed in many conversations I have ever had, but if we are working on a balance of mind, body, and spirit, it is essential that we keep our digestive system operating at its best ability. Roughage is that food which contains indigestible fiber that enhances the ability of the intestines to move solid waste from the body more efficiently. A sluggish colon contributes to many health problems. Entire books have been written on the subject and much is available on some of the internet search engines.

When you are looking to balance the body point on the mind/body/spirit triad every person will have choices and decisions to make on the foods they allow in their daily diet. One only has to look at things like lifestyle to realize that many factors come into play when we make our food choices. If you are working a full time job and raising a family, there will be much less time available for you to prepare food, and you will probably be more likely to pick up fast food to supplement your meals. Most foods that we buy that are not prepared at home with fresh ingredients are loaded with substances that are not going to contribute to a well-balanced body. As scientific research gains more and more information, our decisions about the foods we choose become more and more muddled.

The actual foods we eat also contribute to our overall good health. While there is much controversy over foods that are labeled "organic," those foods by very definition are grown in a manner that contributes less toxicity than those that are not labeled "organic." Knowing this, it becomes easier to choose from all of the choices that are available to us. Learning to read labels and compare ingredients of food that we are not actually preparing ourselves becomes vital if we are to find a healthier diet. The American diet has become so very toxic because we have become consumers of fast foods whether they are found at a drive-thru or whether they are found in a frozen food section in a supermarket. Most of these foods contain excessive amounts of sodium, fat, and/or sugar in some form or another. Keep in mind that sodium is a necessary component, so it is termed a natural ingredient, and it is found naturally in most foods. What we need to be aware of is the amount of sodium that is in the food we consume. If you look at a can of green beans, you can see the huge difference of sodium in a regular can and one that is labeled as having "no salt added." Compare and you will see what I am talking about. This difference can be found in any canned food. If you look at frozen vegetables, you will find that they are frozen without added salt. Knowing this makes frozen vegetables a healthier choice than canned vegetables unless you choose those cans with "no salt added." Freshly grown organic vegetables are the best choice you can make. If you have a small amount of space (even some large pots on a patio) growing your own vegetables is the very best choice.

When we are working on balancing our lives so that we are able to be our best self, it is necessary that we do the research ourselves on nutritional topics as we become concerned about them. I have spent much time researching the effects of dairy foods and foods containing wheat gluten. Because of what I found, I am working on eliminating those items from my food choices as often as I can. I personally have never found foods that I have needed to totally eliminate; I have found many that I need to restrict. Some foods have served as a trigger to my body and I have over - consumed because I have eaten those foods. Because those foods trigger bad choices, I make choices that don't include those foods very often. I have found that any time I tell myself I cannot have something, it is the very thing that hounds me at every corner.

Perhaps you are comfortable with your choices in food but need to concern yourself with portion size. We can choose the very healthiest of ingredients but unless we prepare them in a healthy manner and eat them in an appropriate amount, we will not be making the balanced choices that will contribute to a healthy, balanced life. Adding vast amounts of oil, sugar, sugar substitute, or almost any other ingredient changes a healthy food to an unhealthy food. When fast food restaurants were under the magnifying glass several years ago as being great contributors of unhealthy bodies in children, it was found, through scientific testing, that these foods actually contain the amount of fat, sodium, and sugar that actually ensures that they become addicted and guarantees that a customer will return for those foods. If you have ever gotten into the "habit" of stopping at your favorite fast food restaurant two or three times a week, you can understand this addiction.

In order to contribute to a balanced life, we need to choose healthy foods that are preserved with our health in mind. We need to prepare them in a healthy manner and consume them in healthy portions. When we accept the responsibility for our own bodies and pursue the information that will help us make wise and healthy choices, we contribute to the creation of a more balanced body that will serve to give us a more balanced life. The choices are yours daily.

MOVE IT!!! MOVE IT!!!

Another way in which we balance our lives is through learning to move efficiently. There are many ways to exercise and many benefits of exercise. This is one area of my life that is definitely not in balance because I avoid body movement much too often. Because we owe this physical body so very much, we should be willing to reward it by giving it the very best treatment possible. It is responsible for moving us from place to place. When we do not exercise as we should, our muscular system does not operate as efficiently as it can and our movements often become hindered. If for no other reason than maintaining movement, we need to become aware of the necessity of exercise.

Too often we think of exercise as a way to sculpt our bodies so that they make our body more appealing for others to look at. There is nothing wrong with this motivation, but exercise has a much more beneficial result: to contribute to our ease of movement. The old axiom, "Use it, or lose it," is definitely in order when we consider the benefits of exercise. We have to realize that there are also many different forms of exercise and we can choose from among them for the different contributions they make to our bodies.

Because we are creatures that stand erect and balance our bodies on two feet in order to walk, it is not a surprise that one of the very best exercises is one of the most simple. It is the exercise of walking. When we choose to walk, without stopping, for twenty minutes per day, we have laid claim to one of the most beneficial movements our body can make. Twenty minutes gives us enough time to increase our heart rate so that we have contributed to our cardiovascular health. Walking gives the joints in our legs exercise that will contribute to preserve the fluidity of our movement. It also raises our heart rate sufficiently to increase our metabolism, or burning point, to more efficiently use the food we eat and keep our bodies from storing it as fat. When we combine this form of exercise with a healthy daily diet, we will have a healthy body. Our body will, in its own conscious awareness, settle itself into the healthiest weight for our physical needs. We can maneuver our bodies somewhat by decreasing what is ingested and increasing exercise. When we do this, the body will create a different "set point." Once we have a body that is working at an optimum efficiency, the only thing that is needed is for us to continue with this regimen.

Other exercises can also play a part in our healthy body. Many people want to increase the strength of their muscles and choose to add weight training exercises to their regime. Depending on whether you choose quick movements with lighter weights or slow movements with heavier weights, you can achieve different results. When embarking on weight training, it is important to work with a trainer or someone who knows what movements are necessary to achieve the desired results. Classes in Pilates, Zumba, and Yoga are usually available in most communities and can provide different results for the body. Once again, in order to balance your best self, you are the one who needs to decide what best facilitates your body's health. No one else can make these balancing decisions for you. You will be the one who is responsible for making those decisions for your body, and you are the one who will be using your body in a way that you find to be most convenient and most efficient.

When you are exercising your body, regardless of the kind of exercise you choose, you will be contributing to a healthier lifestyle and all systems of the body will respond to the increased attention you are taking to make it more efficient.

When we consider balance in the way we are discovering the mind/body/spirit connection we need to come up with a plan that can incorporate exercise into our lifestyle. Not everyone has the pocketbook or time frame to make exercise at a gym a possibility. We may have no desire to go to a gym to work out. For exercise to help create a balance it must be something we already enjoy or can learn to enjoy. I put out some money years ago and even sought the help of a trainer so that I would be locked into participation of a plan. I tried to approach it with a positive attitude but failed. The trainer was very nice and encouraging, the exercises were not too difficult, and there was no describable reason it should not have been a pleasant experience, but it wasn't. I did not enjoy one minute of the time spent. I did not look forward to going nor did I feel any sense of satisfaction when the exercise period was over. In other words, it was a bust! I have tried to varying degrees since then to establish a routine I can live with and have repeatedly come up short. I have not given up nor do I intend to. I realize that right now this may be the one overriding factor that is keeping me out of balance and keeping my body from its optimum potential.

Sometimes our life seems out of whack and we are experiencing situations and events that cause us problems in our daily lives. There may be times when only physical activity will give our spirit a way to work out the frustrations and consider alternative ways to deal with those issues. Consider that walking may not be your answer. For you it may be yoga or something of more physically challenging nature like extreme workouts offer. Much will depend upon your physical abilities at the time. Walking does not require this advance preparation. Because I have been living an extraordinarily sedate life for the last couple of years, walking will be my exercise of choice.

WHAT PART DOES FORGIVENESS PLAY?

Another area we need to look at in order to balance the mind/body/spirit connection is that of forgiveness. When we hold with an unforgiving attitude, we are contributing to our own stress. When the body deals with stress, it produces cortisol. Cortisol is the stress hormone that is considered to be one of the major contributors to poor health. Scientists have been telling us for years that increased cortisol levels interfere with learning and memory, lowers immune function, can cause weight gain and increase in blood pressure, cholesterol levels, and can contribute to heart disease.

Knowing these facts, it becomes increasingly important that we rid ourselves of stress as much and as often as possible. When we carry with us unresolved conflict and unresolved issues with others, we are adding to the stress on all of our bodily systems even though we usually don't know it. It is when we forgive others for transgressions against us, either real or imagined, that we gain a release from this stress. All of the systems of our body will respond accordingly. When we forgive someone we are giving ourselves a gift of freedom. If you have an unforgiven issue with, let's say, a parent who is no longer with you, you can still forgive them and release the hold that the lack of forgiveness has on you. One of the most effective ways of doing this is to write a letter to the person. You can even state the reasons you feel the way you do, how their action made you feel, and how you have held this in. Once you have done this part, you can then tell them with all of the love you can muster that even though this is how you once felt that you now are willing to let it go and forgive them. Some people choose to burn the letter and have the smoke and ashes carry the transgression away into the Universe. You can also just release your feelings and give your forgiveness with a prayer stating your forgiveness. Obviously, if the person is still in the physical realm, you will need to either write to them or talk with them. It may not be easy, but it will release so much tension from you once it is done that you will physically feel the difference.

It may be that the person you are forgiving will not accept an apology and your forgiveness. That is no longer your problem; it becomes their problem if they are unwilling to accept the gift of forgiveness you are offering them. The very act of forgiving is a gift to both the one giving the forgiveness and the one receiving the forgiveness. It is the equivalent of an olive branch being offered that can bring peace to both parties. We all have situations that have been created in our lives that have made forgiveness a topic that we would not even consider. I will say, from personal experience, when I forgave those that I had never considered forgiving, I found a peace that had been denied before. Had I not forgiven them, I have no doubts that peace and contentment would have been impossible for me to achieve and enjoy.

Because we are human creatures, we learn behaviors that other animals do not learn. We begin life very innocently and we accept the equality of everyone. As we grow and learn from those around us, we adapt their values as ours. This is where we begin to veer from the path we originally set out on when we became a physical being. As we observe others and their actions and reactions, we make certain assumptions and we react accordingly. We decide who is acceptable of our love and who is not, who is good enough to be our friends and who is not, and what we determine is behaviorally okay and what is not. Because of these assumptions, we are beginning to create our own paths in life. We establish relationships based on our choices, and those people we closely associate with usually share our values. Because we do not possess a great deal of experience in our formative years, we find ourselves stumbling along and making decisions that can create ill will and hurt feelings with others. They also contribute to feelings that cause us to hold them in a place where we resent and dislike them. If we are very lucky, we have mentors who help us work through these problems, and we learn to appropriately deal with our feelings in a way that will help us avoid recreating these problems over and over again.

While we learn acceptable and unacceptable behaviors, we also create a smaller egoic self that feeds us messages that may become counterproductive. While a healthy ego is necessary for establishing our own identity of self, if it is not carefully guarded it can become controlling enough that we lose our unique identity and become much like a sheep led around and herded at the will of others. When this egoic self becomes extremely strong it contributes to keeping us in a holding pattern that does not serve our best self and our best life. We become very interested in comparing ourselves to others and making sure that we come out better than those around us. In order to do this, we use all sorts of behaviors with little regard as to how we are affecting those around us. We no longer care if we hurt someone's feelings or create disruption in other's lives. We become more interested in being right in all situations and controlling others so that our superiority is recognized.

I had a discussion with a friend this morning that serves to illustrate the necessity of forgiveness and how we deal with it in our lives. She was sharing a bit of her life and was discussing how her son, who is in his mid-forties has little to do with her and allows her to see her four grandchildren only a couple of times a year. She raised this young man at a time in her life that was particularly difficult as a single parent and as a functioning alcoholic. She was fighting her demons and at the same time able to keep a job, a roof over their heads and food on the table. She met the demons, faced them down, and came out on the strong side. She has spent the last twenty-five years atoning for those times. As we talked, I could see the pain behind her eyes. She readily admitted that she was not proud of some of the decisions she had made. I pointed out that once she was forgiven for those transgressions and had made the amends to those she had unwittingly hurt, she was not responsible for their reactions. She had done her "soul work." That is all we can do; we cannot control the reactions of others to any situation. We covered many topics, but I think the one of forgiveness is one of the most important. As we are balancing our lives we need to realize that the reaction of others may cause us angst, but it is our own reactions that cause that angst to continue to plague us. None of us can rewrite the past. We are who we are because of those choices previously made. Neither she, nor you, nor I would be who we are had we made different decisions. That in itself is reason enough to be thankful for all of the opportunities that have been placed in our path. **When we forgive ourselves as thoroughly as we do others, we are gaining a great deal of headway in balancing our lives and showcasing our best self.**

All sorts of issues present themselves in life that necessitate our forgiving others, and all sorts of issues requires us to ask to be forgiven. The point that must be remembered is that if we do something that hurts someone else, we need to apologize (which is the flip side of forgiveness). When someone causes us to feel badly, it is critical that we forgive them, whether they request it or not. Forgiveness is so necessary to our balance and our well-being that it should become a habit. When I was young I learned to apologize easily. Not everyone does, but I did. It seems that I was putting my foot in my mouth quite often and learned early on that apologies were necessary. Forgiveness was a totally different story. I would accept an apology if it were offered, but I did not see the necessity for forgiveness unless someone asked for it. When you wait for an apology to offer forgiveness, you may wait a lifetime. While you are waiting for that apology you can waste a lot of your time holding a grudge thereby resisting good things in life that may be trying to come your way.

HOW DO THE ARTS PLAY A PART?

The arts play a significant part in our lives whether we realize it or not. Even the word "art" means many different things to people. It is a human reaction to respond to art in our world, whether we create it or whether we react to it. We think of the art found in museums but there is also the art created by our kindergarten child. Is one more important to our human experience than the other?

Art can refer to either natural beauty or created beauty. It can result from a need to beautify - that is to embellish, adorn, and display - or a need for self-expression. Things that we do for play, such as a game of chess, may not be artful but it can satisfy the need for self-expression; therefore, play can cover the same features of art as can fantasy and make-believe. It is a creative play, as is actual theatre play, which definitely falls into the category of art. There is an art to the creation of textiles as well as how those textiles are used to recreate additional art such as quilts or clothing. Pottery can be created to be either functional or artistic, and what is functional can also be artistic in its creation. Music is art, and it can be created by nature, or it can be created through the use of instruments that have also been artistically created. We do not have to be a certain age to appreciate the creative creation of music. You will note that even babies will respond to the musical voice of their mother as well as the tune of a lullaby. What is now considered art, such as the cave drawings found from prehistoric cultures, were at one time simply functional needs of that culture. We usually accept that something is art when what is considered ordinary is elevated to be considered extraordinary. For the purposes of our balancing needs, we need only accept that any creative expression that soothes our senses is worthy of being called art. If it is soul soothing to dance to the melodic beat of reggae, then that, too, is art.

We can think that we do not need arts to be balanced, but there is evidence to the contrary. If we are to observe babies and toddlers, we will see that from birth they will listen to music and they will vocalize. Without being taught, they will pick up crayons and figure out what to do with them. They kick, wiggle, and smile, all of which are artistic expressions. They also respond to adults when those adults make faces at them and use expressive gestures.

Arts are ever present in human society. Our bodies are art whether we choose tattooing them or adorning ourselves with colorful jewelry and clothing. We choose decorative objects to surround ourselves with in our homes and in our places of worship. We sing, we dance, and we create. So, whether we consider ourselves artistic or not, we are by our very nature artistic. Some respond to the offerings in art museums while others respond to a photograph. It is not the choice of a particular artistic endeavor, but rather the response to any artistic endeavor that tells us that having the arts in our lives is a necessity.

With every expression and interaction, we are creating. We create friendships and relationships. We adorn the lives of others. We move, we sway to the beats we hear, and we appreciate the beauty of a sunset. All of this is art and it is in the appreciation of this naturally occurring art, in the response to this art, that we are balancing ourselves. When we fail to "take time to smell the roses," we are disallowing art to help keep us balanced. We can use the arts to our advantage by allowing ourselves to simply appreciate. Appreciate that talent, the expression, the sharing, and the immensity of focus presented by the creator, and draw from that to add to our own lives. I may not, personally, find the work of Picasso to be something I eagerly anticipate seeing. I can appreciate that it was his means of creative expression and as such is worthy of some degree of appreciation simply as an art form.

Another point we need to consider when discussing the arts is that we have probably all been presented with what we consider to be the "right" way and the "wrong" way to express ourselves. If we were taught that a painted picture needs to be an accurate image of a scene or a person, then naturally, as in the example of Picasso, we may dismiss it more easily. It was not until I took an art appreciation class in college (that was required, naturally) that I became more appreciative of all of the artistic movements. Suddenly a different world opened up to me because the boundaries of "acceptable" and "unacceptable" were broadened and I was able to widen my frames of reference. The more we allow ourselves to enjoy what was previously unacceptable, the more we are able to balance our emotions, our ego, and our soul. We then take this broadened acceptance of the arts and transfer it to other areas of our lives. Because we are more accepting of different types of music, art, poetry, fiction, etc., the more we accept individuals who differ from us in the scope of their beliefs, gender, nationality, and race, etc. The more we learn, accept, and appreciate on any level of the arts, the more easily we can balance that mind/body/spirit connection that we have.

Another aspect of the arts that needs to be considered and explored is that of creativity. When we begin listing what can keep us in balance, we find that one of the prime needs of man is to create. We are a creation of the source that most people call God. Because we are a part of the creator, it is an intrinsic part of us to create. That is what we do. That is what we need to do in order to fulfill the most basic of our needs.

Creating comes naturally to us. We do not have to create symphonies or works of art worthy of a museum to be a creator. Everything we do is a creation. When we make something from nothing, we have played the role of the creator. This is our purpose: to create. What we call God is more than we can realize. God cannot be divided so the essence of us is that of God. The only way that God can experience anything is through our individual experiences. Because "he" cannot be divided, that means that our experiences are his. The universe expands through the daily choices and experiences each of us have.

A friend and I have had some very interesting conversations lately as we have discussed what Wallace Wattles discussed about the creative space. There is, within all of us, that creative space. When we attach our energy to that space, we create. If we deny or ignore or override that energy, we do not create. When two people who have a very energetic, almost chemical, connection, that energy is multiplied many times over. The creation becomes more metaphysically possible because of the magnificence of the added energy. When two people who have a physical attraction channel that energy, or love, into a creative endeavor rather than a physical union, the resulting creative effort is   mind-bending. When we look at this in a mind/body/spirit connection, one can see that a relationship based on energetic love that is not acted upon physically (i.e. sexually) is probably one of the most creative uses of energy as well as the most productive.

IS THERE A DIFFERENCE BETWEEN APPRECIATION AND GRATITUDE?

This is a relatively simple question but it does not have a simple answer. We use the terms interchangeably and that is perfectly okay. When we start digging a bit deeper we find that the difference is a result of the underlying thoughts and feelings that are associated with both words. Gratitude usually results from being grateful for something in our life. Just because we are grateful doesn't always mean that we appreciate what we have. Gratitude, therefore, can be thought of as something that leads to appreciation. Going from gratitude to appreciation usually requires us to be more mindfully aware of the reasons we are grateful to begin with.

As I researched sources to accurately convey the differences, the example that showed up more than once was food. We can be grateful there is food on our table, but to go further we can appreciate it for not only its taste, but also for the fragrance and nutrition that comes with it. Gratitude is felt after you get what you want. You can't always get what you want, and this is where appreciation enters. You appreciate what you have been given even if it is not quite what you have asked for. We move beyond gratitude and recognize other values that are added to our lives as a result.

While I took a bit of liberty with this, it was found on the Goddess-Body-Mind-Spirit.com website, with an article by Tirra-Olufemi who expresses very well that there is a power in gratitude. We are able to transcend any sense of victimhood (I am too fat, I am not smart enough, I am poor, etc.) and begin to take back ownership of our power. The power in appreciation is that we are already in our power and seeking to use it consciously and deliberately. We can be grateful to be employed but that does not mean that we appreciate the job we have. Evelyn Lim and Abraham Hicks also compare the attitude of gratitude and appreciation when discussing the contributions of both to our vibrations. Lim reiterates that although they are used interchangeably, the difference they offer in our vibration is what defines them differently. Abraham tells us time and time again that appreciation carries the same energetic vibration as love and it reflects the absence of fear and resistance. Gratitude carries the residue of past struggles that we have overcome. While gratitude causes us to express our thanks, appreciation is coming from a more natural feeling from within. Appreciation is about bringing what we are grateful for into a more mindful knowing. It is much more expansive in scope. If gratitude were expressed by a rose bud, appreciation would be the rose in full bloom.

We can practice appreciation in several ways. As we move from gratitude to appreciation, we raise our vibrations in a way that will help us balance our lives. Five ways to help us along this path are as follows:

1. Practice gratitude NOW. We focus on the present and realize that we are already enjoying many blessings. As we concentrate on gratitude, we find more and more to be grateful for and before you realize it, you are approaching appreciation.

2. Be authentic to your feelings. If you express gratitude verbally but do not feel it within, you need to stop lying to yourself. Your vibrations respond only to your feelings, not your words.

3. Connect with your feelings. Your vibration goes up when you experience those positive emotions.

4. Everything counts. Be thankful as you have your cup of coffee or you do your laundry. Be thankful for everything. Once you begin to notice the beauty in even the smallest things, you will find your life changing.

5. Make it part of your daily routine. Live your life in an attitude of gratitude and you will find the more you are grateful, the sooner you will become appreciative.

As we use these words and emotions as a way to balance the mind/body/spirit connection, we need to remember that the underlying vibration is often very different, and it is this difference that we need to recognize. When we feel grateful for something it is often because we have come through something negative to get to that point. Even though you are focused on feelings of gratitude, you mind may be dragging up some of the back story and the negative feelings that correspond to the energy felt at that time. When you are able to shift from gratitude to appreciation, that history is no longer attached to those feelings. When we realize the subtle differences, we can actually practice feeling appreciative in all sorts of ways. One of my easiest ways to be appreciative is to indulge in the wonders of nature. As we become more accustomed to those feelings of appreciation, we will be able to slide into that vibration more easily... If there is ever a choice to feel grateful or to feel appreciation, always choose appreciation.

Once we understand the difference and work on going from gratitude to appreciation, much of our battles with the situations in our lives cease to exist. Those problems that still plague us become more insignificant and thus, more manageable. The easiest way I have found to get into a feeling of appreciation occurs when I simply look up into the sky. Whether it is night or day, when we confront the magnificence of the atmosphere, we realize in our insignificance, we are powerful. To consider that in all of the immensity of the Universe we are here, we realize that we have a reason and a purpose to being here. We may not know yet what that purpose is, but we can no longer doubt that we do have a purpose. This feeling creates within me a knowing that while my ego may be trying to keep me tethered to earthly beliefs, my soul acknowledges my importance. In that knowing, there is a flood of appreciation from within my heart. This is the kind of appreciation of myself that encourages the love and appreciation of everyone and everything. Any time that our supposed "reality" hits us, we only need to do those things that bring that feeling of appreciation to us, and we will be back in the vibrations that exist to make our best self the only reality we need.

Author Melody Beattie tells us, "Gratitude unlocks the fullness of life. It turns what we have into enough, and more. It turns denial into acceptance, chaos to order, confusion to clarity. It can turn a meal into a feast, a house into a home, a stranger into a friend. Gratitude makes sense of our past, brings peace for today, and creates a vision for tomorrow." It is from this platform that we begin to appreciate all that life has to offer.

MOTIVATION OR INSPIRATION

When reading some of the works of Dr. Wayne Dyer a few years ago, I recall that he stated that while he was known as a motivational speaker, he hoped he was actually an inspirational speaker. Motivation comes from being given a choice to follow and inspiration is simply a calling to be who you are meant to be, who you really are. Motivation is a good starting point. There are many times in our life that we seem to be stuck. We are at a place of stagnation but we have no idea how to get to there (where we think we want to be) from here (where we are). It is at a time like this that a dose of motivation is very helpful. We look to the lives of those around us, talk to others who have achieved something similar to what we hope for, and make decisions from a place of learning. This is what motivation is all about. It is what leads us to serve as role models. This is why public servants like teachers, police personnel, and firefighters are often thought of as being individuals that young people want to aspire to become. We now have the class of celebrities such as rock stars and sports figures that also serve as role models. When we are considering motivation, it becomes necessary to ask ourselves if the models are going toward the kind of values we hope the next generation emulates or whether they are veering too far from the ideal. At this point in history, there is an incredible amount of self-serving, self-absorbed posturing going on by many individuals.

When we view these same individuals as a source of inspiration rather than motivation, the qualities of their life and their life choices becomes more important. When it is the "idea" of being a firefighter that consumes a young person, the value that a firefighter provides to the betterment of society provides the "inspiration". We understand through this illustration the meaning of the differences in the two words.

There are many vocational and professional choices where the differences become crystal clear. If you are ever in hospital being treated for an illness, the difference is noticeable. You will readily understand the difference when you are being assisted by a nurse who is inspired to that choice of career and the person who is motivated by what that career provides them. When we come from a place of motivation, we are more in tune to the external circumstances of the particular choice. It is when we are inspired to a choice of our life's work that we realize that there was no other path for us, it is who we are. The inspiration/motivation factor does not just exist in the job market. We see inspiration in the choices of flowers one may use around their garden. We may see inspiration in the interior arrangement of furniture, and we can see inspiration in the meals we create. Inspiration results in the internal desire to share who we are in any way we can with those around us. While motivation to be better today than yesterday is not problematic in any way, it cannot compete for inspiration in how it makes us and those around us feel.

We may be leading a very inspired (in-spirit) life yet there are times we may still respond to motivation. The reverse is also true. We may be very motivated in our behavior but lack the inspiration needed to take our lives to the next level. When we consider the balances in our lives, we usually refer to the things that motivate us. What may motivate us to seek a new job at one point in our life is not the same motivation to seek a different job at a different time in our life. We may, at the age of twenty-two, be looking for a rewarding career and become motivated to get the education necessary for that career. Later in life, at say thirty-eight, we may have become disillusioned with the previous choice, we may be in the midst of a divorce and contemplating the loss of income that divorce involves and look at a direction that will give us greater financial resources. When we reach the age of sixty-five, we may look at a job that will supplement our pension income. Our motivations are different at each stage of our lives. When we think of our lives in light of inspiration, we may, for example, take the field of education. Given the same set of circumstances above, if we are living a life of inspiration, we will continue to seek opportunities in the field of education for no other reason than we cannot imagine our lives in any other way. The venue may be different; however the direction will be the same simply because we come from a place of inspired living.

When we depend upon motivation to guide our lives, we can become out of balance simply because those motivations come from without rather than within. They are subject to our different whims on a given day. When we turn from motivation and embrace an inspired life, we bring that balance back into check. I have been motivated to lose large amounts of weight twice in my lifetime. As the pounds began creeping back up after the second time, I realized that I was relying on something outside to motivate me. What I learned was that I need to believe in myself enough to be inspired to live a healthy lifestyle, one that will not need motivation to keep my weight/size in check. I will be inspired to eat healthy foods, to exercise in a way that encourages a healthy body, and to live as an example for others, simply because I can.

While everyone's path is different, there are some parallels in life as we choose our options. When I look at someone who has fought a weight/size battle and is gaining control of their body, I am inspired. When I keep my body in check, I am, in turn, inspiring others. When we view our lives in a way that encourages us to be an inspiration to others, we lose the need for external motivation. These are choices we make daily. Whatever we decide to do is okay, it really doesn't matter in the grand scheme of things. We are okay, regardless. When we consider balance to our lives, however, it becomes a different way to look at life. Inspiration is more personal and intense than motivation. When we inspire others, we are living at a higher vibration of satisfaction than when we are waiting and waiting for something to motivate us externally. I get this way quite often regarding exercise. I wait and wait to be motivated and when it doesn't happen, I give up. What we need to realize is that a month later, or a year later, that time will have passed, regardless of our choices, and where will we be in what we want for our lives? **When we make decisions that come from inspiration rather than motivation, we are gaining the impetus to make our lives the best they can be.**

Well, that sounds well and good, you think but what if I have physical limitations? It doesn't matter. You are inspired to make choices for yourself at whatever your level is.

REASONS OR EXCUSES?

Perhaps there is a valid reason that a person does not participate in strenuous exercise classes. It is a valid reason, but it should not be an excuse. There are some exercises that are within the reach of most people. When we choose to use our excuses as our reasons, we are definitely throwing ourselves out of balance. When I do this, I am telling myself several things. I am saying that I am incapable, that I am somehow inept, and that I am undeserving. None of these statements are reflective of who I really am and they all are keeping me from acknowledging my best self. Keep in mind, that "my best self" is exactly who I decide that I am going to be. It is not dependent upon who you are and what you can do. It is not dependent upon how you look or how you dress. My best self occurs when I am living my own life in a way that I deem is right for me. If I choose to accept that I will not exercise, that is okay, but I cannot say it is okay on one hand and bemoan the fact that I am having difficulty with my movement on the other hand. It is one way or it is the other way. I am the only one who can decide.

When we get all motivated in the spring to get ourselves toned up for swimsuit season, we get started on some exercise plan and get really excited about it. After a couple of weeks or a month, we miss a class, then we miss another one, and sooner or later we are moaning over the fact that the exercise plan did not work. This works in every aspect of our lives. We start on a project and quit before it is done and wonder why others seem to be so creative and we do not. The major factor is that they don't give up on themselves. They don't expect perfection. They allow that the project will take time and effort on their part. They immerse themselves in the project, and it becomes an extension of who they are. One year I was inspired to create nine quilts to give to my children, grandchildren, and a couple of close friends for Christmas. I was inspired almost to the point of mania, but I literally could not go a day without working on one of those quilts. Because of the intensity of my experience, once they were done it has become difficult for me to reach that level of intensity for quilting again. I burned out. I over achieved and in that overachievement, I decided that I did not want that level of mania again. I find that my desire for balance is sometimes difficult because I tend to approach every aspect of my life in this way. I am either all or nothing in my approach. Now, I can use this as a reason or an excuse.

I can face the fact that this is a part of my personality. This does not mean anything, in and of itself. So what? What it does allow me to do is to embrace this part of me as being okay. If I use this minute portion of what makes me Nancy, as an excuse, it can cripple me when I attempt any project. If I use this as an excuse, I can keep using it over and over when I am striving to deliver my best self and it will serve to, once again, let my ego have the ammunition to convince me that I am incapable of completing whatever the project is for whatever reason it wants to. Perhaps one project cannot be completed because I don't have the time, and one because I don't have the information needed, and one because I don't have the skill. My all-or-nothing-ness will continue to serve as an excuse as long as I allow it.

When I face this part of my personality as the reason, rather than the excuse, it will let me work around this reason and find other ways to continue with the project I am beginning. When you convert your excuses to reasons, there is very little that you cannot accomplish. It may require you to make changes in your schedule, to get a greater skill set, or to gain more knowledge. The fact remains that it will no longer keep you from achieving what it is that you are trying to achieve. This one bit of information can make worlds open up. When the doors open, there is a flood of experiences that you can enjoy that you were denying yourself. As long as your goal is one that you can believe that you are capable of achieving, you can achieve it. You may realize that, if, for example, you want to make a quilt but you have never sewn before, it will take time to learn the necessary skills. Throw those desires out to the Universe and the Universe will take care of the details, if we let it.

When we give up our hold on all of the excuses we use, we will be amazed at how our lives unfold. As in my other books, I will refer you to one of the ultimate books that addressed this issue for me was, "Excuses, Begone!" by Dr. Wayne Dyer. It was enjoyable to read and became an invaluable tool for me as I began my journey. I still refer to it when I get headed in a direction that is opposite where I want to go. When I begin to see that I am using an excuse to keep a goal away from me, I get his book out, read it, and find that I am headed back in the right direction. When we realize that we are off balance, we are in a wonderful place to begin rebalancing ourselves. This is an ongoing process. **Our enjoyment of our life is worth so much more than the excuses we use to keep us from that best life and from our best self.**

A valuable exercise is to just begin listing all of the things that you want in life. Do this with a brainstorming effort and hold nothing back. No desire is too outrageous for this exercise. No desire is too unrealistic. After the list is made, go back and ask yourself why it is that you have not already achieved this particular item. Very often our desires change. I thought at one time in my life that I would like to go skydiving. I did not want this enough to pursue it. I know this because I also wanted to cruise the Mediterranean Sea and see some of the Greek Isles. I wanted this enough that I accomplished it. The difference is the intensity of our desires. Some of our desires never change, and as we begin working on that "bucket list" of desires, the list will change. When you begin pursuing those desires, you will need to see which ones are being kept away because of what you are using as an excuse. Is it a reason (which can be addressed and dealt with) or is it simply an excuse (which is most often an invalid assumption on the part of the ego)?

As I deal with the reason/excuse conundrum in my own life I begin to realize that most of the time I have been kept away from my desires it has been because of excuses created by my ego. I have listened to others who have told me the goal is not within my reach, and I have chosen to believe them. I have a friend who announced recently that she will be taking flying lessons. That is an admirable goal but I find it rather strange because this same individual refused to fly until a few weeks ago, with the help of medication. This has never been in the realm of desire in this person's life. While I find it to be a strange goal on her part, I applaud that she is making the effort to achieve this desire and I wish her well. Her example serves to reinforce the fact that our goals change constantly. When we have a true desire and we allow others to convince us that we are incapable of achieving it, we will find ourselves regretting that decision at some point. When you have a desire, and it is a strong desire, find a way to achieve it and do not allow anyone or anything to cause you to use anything as an excuse to keep you away from that achievement.

When we consistently deny ourselves the opportunity to live an authentic life, we find at the end of this physical life that we will have regrets. Those regrets will most assuredly be from the things that were left undone, rather than regrets of what we did enjoy. Turn away from excuses. Use your reasons as a legitimate concern then work to find a way to resolve that concern. This will make what you previously felt to be unachievable come in your realm of enjoyment. Try it, and I think you find it holds one of the keys to balancing your best self.

FIND A WAY TO ENJOY ALL OF YOUR EXPERIENCES

I do not go to the doctor very often. For the most part I am blessed with good health and I appreciate that very much. Recently I noticed that my left knee was larger than my right knee and I was experiencing occasional twinges of discomfort. I kept an eye on this and after a couple of months decided I probably should go to get a professional opinion. I appreciated the gorgeous day and the presence of a fine orthopedic center with doctors trained to diagnose all sorts of medical conditions. The staff was pleasant and helpful. The x-ray technician was friendly and the experience was quite nice. When the doctor came in I was given news that could be taken one of two ways. It was either going to be good news or bad news. Actually, the bad news of an arthritic flare was the good news of an arthritic flare. We can choose to turn bad news into good news any time we choose to. In this case, it was not difficult to do because I did not consider that I had received any bad news. I was aware that I had touches of arthritis already, I had just never experienced the swelling that can accompany it. I will take some medicine for inflammation for a time and if that does not help, a shot will be available. Good news all around.

It is not always this easy to turn our experiences around to enjoyment, but it can be done and when it is, we will experience a sense of relief. When we experience relief, we are giving up feelings of apprehension and anxiety, and we are allowing less resistance to a bountiful life. The more often that we can enjoy an experience, the higher our vibrations will be, and the higher our vibrations, the more enjoyment we will continue to experience. It is a cyclical occurrence, and the benefits to your emotional and physical health will be noticeable.

Becoming our best self is an eye-opening experience. Because you are reading this, you have probably already discovered and embraced your best self. Once you realize who you are and the power that is encapsulated in your very existence, it is easy to become complacent. You can feel that because you have discovered your significance that it will just cause you to glide along in perfection. This is not the case. Our lives are not lived in a vacuum. Energy is all around us, indeed we are part of that energy ourselves. Look around you and you will see that what existed one hundred years ago is often unavailable to us in our life today. What worked for our parents does not work for us in a day to day appreciation of life. We have technology and intelligence available in this decade that did not exist even ten years ago. There is very little, externally, that does not change. What we can count on are those things that occur within. The one thing that we can always count on is love. I am not speaking of the romantic kind of love, or even any kind of love from others, but rather the appreciation- of- all- of- life's- experience's-kind of love. It is the kind of love that allows you to appreciate the rainy day as well as the sunny day. It is the kind of love that doesn't shun others because you are having a "bad hair" day. It is the kind of love that only you are able to give to yourself, that total acceptance of everything exactly as it is. That is the kind of love that will enable you to enjoy every experience.

You will find this approach to life to be extremely refreshing. When you no longer base your value or anyone else's value on a prescribed decision made by society, you will be free. Your life will be balanced. Your body, your mind, and your spirit will be in total agreement. This freedom will be closer to your reality the more you turn all of your experiences into events of enjoyment. Now we will get down to the brass tacks of how this evolution can come about for each of us.

Draw an experience into your mind. I will use an experience I had when I was about to leave town to visit my daughter and granddaughter who live about a five hour drive away from me. I noticed that I was having a problem with my headlights. If I were going to be at home, I could simply avoid driving at night and take my time in getting my car to get it fixed. That was not the case this time however. I was leaving town in two days and needed to get this fixed quickly. I asked the man who changes my oil for a suggestion of where I could go to get it fixed and was referred to an auto shop not far from where I lived. I choose to accept the situations and simply not allow myself to get tense over what the problem "might" be. It turned out to be rather insignificant and easily fixed. During this time the mechanic found a weak battery and also replaced it. I was thrilled. I could have grumbled about the necessity of having to take my car in, the expense of getting it fixed, the additional expense of the battery, etc. I did not do that. I appreciated that I found a reliable reference. I appreciated that it was easily and readily fixed. I appreciated that an additional potential problem was taken care of. I realized that in the fixing of the problem a more difficult problem was waylaid. I allowed myself to take what would have previously been an opportunity for irritation and turned it into a time of appreciation. While it may not have been what we would consider enjoyable in some sense, it was enjoyable in others. It was an experience that resulted in relief; therefore, was an enjoyable experience. Much like my experience at the orthopedic center, it was allowed to be as enjoyable as it could be under the circumstances of its existence.

Using the experience that you drew forth, begin to look at it in a different way. What was the experience? How did you feel about it at the time? How do you feel about it now? Has the elapse of time caused you to feel differently? Could you have viewed the way you looked at it when it happened so that it would have been more enjoyable at that time? If this same experience were to express itself again, could you shift your view so that it would be more enjoyable? Now, to do some pre-planning, is there anything coming up that you are dreading? Is it an actual dread or an imagined dread? Is there any way you can adjust your view of the upcoming event so that you will dread it less? Can you even find a way to appreciate parts of the experience? These are the kinds of practices that you can embrace so that you will reach what is necessary to enjoy your experiences more regularly.

We can take any experience and allow it to morph into something more enjoyable. I can take my time of solitude and by the way I look at it have a totally different experience of it. I can look at is as a lonely and sad time bereft of accompanying presence of others, or I can appreciate it as the time of solitude and renewal of spirit that is only allowed to us when we are alone. I choose to respect and revere my time of solitude and treat it with the appreciation that it deserves. Do I always embrace my solitude in this way? No. Sometimes I seek the company of others, and that is as is should be if we are discussing balance in our lives.

Balance can only exist when we are aware of the differences that experiences will afford us. To explain this further, there are times when I am alone and it bothers me. When this happens, I can allow it to eat away at me and cause me to feel "lonely" or I can choose to do an activity that requires me to do something by myself. I can also use this time to indulge in something that I enjoy, such as music of my choosing or a scented candle that I enjoy. What I choose might be something that I would not be able to enjoy if there were someone else around. That would require a compromise if it involved others. Another thing that solitude affords us is to choose the temperature of our surroundings, that is, we can set our furnace or air conditioner at a temperature that suits us. Solitude allows us to indulge in our life in any way we wish. It is a contemplative time and it a time of refreshment and renewal. We are the directors, producers, and stars of our life when we live in solitude, but we often find that we need to experience something different. We often need to be with others so that we can appreciate the solitude. The opposite can be said also. We may be living a life full of activity and schedules and we have adjusted accordingly but we long for some time to ourselves. When we get time to ourselves, we cannot process it very well because we are so unused to it. If we are to be balanced in life, we need to experience variety so that we can decide what we prefer. There are times in our life where our preferences are not always available to us. We can decide to appreciate where life has led us or to protest. **When we protest our current circumstances, we are self-defeating. Another of the keys to living a balanced life is to be able to adjust to whatever circumstances present themselves with as much grace and ease as we possibly can.** We do this for our own peace and enjoyment, no one else's.

When we listen to the grumblings of others and agree with their assessment, we are throwing ourselves off balance. What balances me will not balance you and visa-versa. If I let what you find to be enjoyable dictate what I enjoy, I will be living your life, not my own. We do this over and over in life. We find something we would like to try, but we are talked out of it. We are in a situation that we can shrug off, but we listen to others and decide that there is more to it and become disgruntled. We sometimes describe someone as "listening to the beat of a different drummer," and this is a reference to someone who chooses to react to circumstances on their own terms. Listening to our own self, our best self, is one of the ultimate gifts we can give ourselves. Two quotes occur to me here: "To thy own self be true," and "The truth shall set you free." **When we follow the beat of our own drum and hold ourselves to our own truth as we experience it, we shall indeed be free and also in balance.**

INTERACTION OF EGO AND PERSONALITY FOR BALANCE

I am involved in a group of meetings that are helping me understand my personality type and the types of others in an effort to more easily interact with and understand those I meet. In a very informal assessment, I was found to possess the personality of "the boss." This label does not surprise me because I spent over thirty years in a classroom doing just that, bossing. While I can accept this as being a major part of my personality, I understand that it is not the only aspect of my personality. None of us are a sum total of one personality type. At various times we will exhibit other personality traits. Within every personality trait, there is also a sliding scale from what is considered the best part of that personality down to the rather undesirable parts of that personality. Our personalities are set when we are young by the set of circumstances, conditions, and personalities that we interact with before we are old enough to know what is happening. While I can accept that my basic personality is that of a boss, I can endeavor to exhibit the best part of that personality type which is "self-confident and decisiveness," rather than the more undesirable parts such as being "willful and confrontational." Each personality type has these sorts of options. I say option, because we do choose our reactions to situations, regardless of personality type.

There are all sorts of tests that will help you to understand the different personality types. The most common may be the Briggs-Myers (or Myers-Briggs, depending on the Internet source you refer) formula that is based on research by Carl Jung. Once you complete this questionnaire, you will get a 4-letter type formula that can then be compared to the personality type assigned to that particular design. You can also find where you stand in the 9 Corporate Personality test. There are tests that have sixteen personality types and those that have only four. In the meetings I am attending, I am using an enneagram, and from what I understood, it is not the only template out there for this type of personality typing either.

We were given additional information to use in the form of homework. We were further cautioned to take care that we not try to match our actions to the type, and attempt to "prove" our type was true, but rather to "catch ourselves" in the acts that are appropriate to that type. Anytime we are given a chance to learn more about ourselves, it is a good idea to take advantage of what is offered.

The next three sessions went on to discuss and pinpoint the different personality types. Some group members took an online questionnaire that some that led them to a closer idea of their personality type and allowed them to fine- tune their original assumption. In addition to learning the traits of the personalities, we also learned behaviors that they would never participate in, which gave additional understanding of the types. The more we delved into the details of the personality types, the more everyone acknowledged that they had friends and family members who flit into the different categories and realized that conflict was often no more than a simple misunderstanding and interaction with their personality traits. It was also observed that we all contain bits and pieces of every type, but there will usually be one overriding type that will be ours.

As we discuss personality, it is our personality that contributes to our outward actions. Those traits are usually what create a default reaction for many of our problems, issues, or situations in general. To be aware is to recognize these tendencies but not to use them as an excuse for our behaviors. Once again, we are reminded of the difference between a reason and an excuse. While our personality type may be the reason we react as we do to a situation, we cannot allow it to become an excuse for poor choices on our part. Poor choices deny our best self the opportunity to shine.

There are characteristics that showcase both the best and worst attributes of any of the personality types that any of the tests provide for us. It is up to us as to how we, personally, will use the personality that we have developed to our betterment. When we have a trait that is not particularly one we desire to embrace, we can see where the ego can help us or hinder us. Take, for example, the "confrontational" trait that is inherent in "the boss" personality that I have. I will not deny that I possess this trait. If my ego is in charge, that trait becomes rampant because that ego insists that I am "right." Because my ego is prodding that trait along, I react in a confrontational way with anyone who disagrees with me. I have such a need to be right (as the ego persists) that I will embrace that characteristic to enforce what the ego has convinced me I need to do in order to be true to that type. When I react in this way, I keep running into conflict. When the ego is in full force, the personality melds with the ego in such a way that confrontation is about the only response available. When you have supervisors who are in a constant state of confrontation with employees, you will recognize that their ego is in charge. When we are aware of this, we can make the changes we need to make to balance this trait out and it will become complacent. If we have done our soul work, we have already seen the damage that our egos can create and we have adjusted our egoic needs accordingly. As a "boss" type who has already made adjustments to the desires of the ego, I find that the aforementioned confrontation mode becomes almost non-existent. I no longer have a need to be "right." Because I don't have this need, the confrontational aspect of my personality has no reason or desire to engage. It becomes benign.

As your ego work and your soul work are embraced, you will find balances in the mind/body/soul connection to become easier and easier to achieve. Life becomes more peaceful and the joy that you had once only hoped to find is becoming more available to you on a daily basis. You are achieving balance.

This kind of work is needed anytime we interact with others regardless of our personality type and their personality type. Using another type, such as the "individualist" the spectrum goes from the positive trait of expressive to the not so great trait of temperamental. If we are allowing our ego to call the shots, we view our temperamental trait as a positive rather than a negative when we are dealing with others. Our ego convinces us that if we draw on this temperamental trait that we can wear others down and get our way in the interaction. In other words, if we are temperamental enough, we will be deemed "right." Once again, the fight for right is the underlying cause of heated interactions in most cases. If you are in a business or job where you interact with many people on a daily basis and their cooperation is necessary for the success of your endeavor, it is wise that you study the personality types and look at yourself and your ego more closely so that these confrontations are kept at a minimum.

When we realize that someone can be confrontational, temperamental, possessive, complacent, or any of the other lower based traits, we can work more effectively with them provided that we are able to call upon our more positive traits to balance them out. When both parties work from their better traits amazing creations and relationships can result.

I WANT TO WIN, DAMMIT!

When we are babies and we are playing, we are given a lot of attention when we grab ahold of the ball for the first time or when we stand for the first time. We are encouraged to get the ball from others and put it in the hoop. We learn strategies to win at Old Maid. We become creatures who find our endorsement in winning. As we grow older, it becomes more evident as we vie for a better job or more recognition in an area of interest. We enter contests and we take classes to perfect our skills, all with the same intent, winning. This becomes hard wired into our very self, or so we think. When we keep our eye on the prize rather than enjoying the journey along the way, we become extremely off balance. The questions then becomes how we can balance our desire for winning with our ego. It can be done but in order to do it, we have to be willing to adjust our view of several things.

We sometimes need to look at the contest more closely. What is it we are trying to do? What is the prize? Is a win worth any strife that may be caused? How important is it to my life's journey that I win this particular battle? You can list any conflict or concern you have and apply these four questions to it. After listing the concern and tackling the four questions, you can then ask yourself, "What need of mine does winning this fulfill?" If you cannot answer this last question with certainty, then it is probably not worth the fight. If this issue is one that in the winning will satisfy either your body's needs, your mind's needs, or your soul's needs, then it is a worthy battle. If it does not connect to the mind/body/spirit balance, then it is pandering to the ego. When we pander to the needs of the ego, we are creating conflict and ignoring our triage of needs for balance.

We have been conditioned and reconditioned in our society to win, win, and win. We have sports figures commanding millions of dollars in salaries to encourage our competitive spirit. We turn all sorts of events into competitions. We applaud the winners and turn away from those who do not come in at the top of the contest. We create winners and therefore we create losers. We make the winners feel absolutely great and the losers feeling lower than snail slime. This causes some to have a feeling of superiority and entitlement while others allow this loser mentality that has been forced upon them by society to permeate all aspects of their life. If you are a winner, you can still be a winner and not perpetuate this senseless trend.

Those who fall into the category of "winners" have a responsibility befall them by the very nature that they are in this category. Noblesse Oblige is the term once used that referred to the obligations of the nobility to serve those less fortunate and help take care of them in life. The winners in the peerage had that responsibility. Until the 21st century, the very wealthy in the world had this sense of obligation also. While there are still many who adhere to this tradition, there are more and more of the uber-wealthy who are pandering to their ego and continue taking, taking, and taking without giving in return. It appears to work for them, but they are throwing themselves more and more off balance and one day it will catch up with them in some way. Let me be clear in this part of the discussion: there is absolutely nothing wrong with working toward a goal and achieving it. There is nothing with wanting to win a contest. It is how it is won that makes the difference in whether you maintain your balance in life. If you are coming from a desire to showcase your best self, you are coming from a balanced effort. If you are coming from a desire to win just to say that you have won, you are coming from an egocentric base, and it will not serve to maintain balance.

We covered the winning aspect. Now for the "losers." If you have placed yourself in the battle, you are not a loser. I was never a fan of physical activity. When we would have team sports, I was picked way down the line, especially when someone who was not a close friend was the captain of the team. I felt like a loser because I was not competent in very many sports. If it was an academic contest, I fared much better, and my inadequacies were negligible. I still shun physical team activities but for a different reason. I don't enjoy them. I have never felt a need to prove myself in the realm of the team sport type activity. I don't put myself in that game. I am neither a winner nor a loser. It causes me no imbalance because it is neutral in my regard.

No one is a loser in every category. I remember watching The Andy Griffith Show. In that series, Gomer Pyle was about as close to a loser as we could have when he first entered the show, if we judged him by the standards that society imposes upon us all. It was during one show where they were looking for a singer to help them win a contest against Mt. Pilot that Gomer showcased his voice. The singing ability of Jim Nabors was launched, and Gomer Pyle achieved a degree of respect in Mayberry that he had not previously been accorded. Everyone has some kind of talent, some area in which they excel, we only have to find it. This is a fictional story but it is indicative of what any of us are capable of. In all fairness to Gomer, he was loved by everyone in Mayberry regardless of his abilities or inabilities because he was always ready to come to the aid of any of his friends. He certainly was no loser in the friend department. We can also look to the fictional character of George Bailey for more instances of the winner vs loser battles. The point is, when we show up in this life, at birth, we are stepping into a physical place where we will be given many opportunities to expand ourselves and find those opportunities that give us joy. When we can see this as part of the journey and not a test in and of itself, we can put it in the perspective in which it belongs.

If you are given the opportunity to influence children, always find ways to encourage them. Do not let them repeatedly be placed in a position to feel like a loser. It is difficult in many instances for us, as adults, not to let situations overwhelm us. Can you imagine the angst and imbalance created for the seven or eight-year- old child just getting into the swing of this life here on earth? Help them create that place of joy within themselves at an early age and you will be balancing your life in the process.

Now that we have examined winners and losers, we need to look at how we choose these individuals. By what criteria is one deemed to be a winner? How important is it that a person be a skilled athlete, or a renowned actor, or a famous political figure? Is it important to our life's journey and to the discovery of our best self that we indulge in what society creates? If our experiences lead us to wanting to be a skilled athlete because we have a deep desire to be an athlete, then we are achieving a balance when we pursue that skill. If we pursue that skill for the fame, the glory, and the money alone, we are off balance. The factors that are behind the pursuit are what causes us to experience the balance or imbalance. What starts as a true desire in any pursuit can begin with purity and can become something that is different. We can love a sport, for example, and once we taste a bit of the fame and glory, we become seduced by it and can want more and more. When this desire for more and more begins, we have turned away from the original goal because the ego has gained a greater hold on our psyche.

Once again, there is nothing wrong with fame and money, it is when this overwhelming desire for glory enables us to think only of those things that we become out of balance. Many singers' and actors' lives serve as grave reminders of what fame and glory can do to a person when the desire to share their gift morphs into a constant struggle to keep themselves at the top of their chosen craft. I don't need to point out examples of this kind of descent because we hear about those weekly. One example of a famous balanced life is that of Paul Newman. Once considered the greatest box office draw of his time, he aged with grace. He and his wife, Joanne Woodward, also an actor, established charitable works that were funded by their salad dressing recipes. I have simplified their story greatly but it serves as the example needed to prove that fame can be a positive factor rather than a negative one. The key is to keep the desires, and results of those desires, in balance mentally, physically, and spiritually.

Recently it was announced that J.K. Rowlings, the author of the Harry Potter books, had lost her status as a billionaire because she had donated so much of her earnings to charity. She had struggled and struggled early in her life and her fame allowed her a venue in which she could share her abundance. She decided when enough was enough and made the decision to share it. She was making a conscious decision to maintain, or perhaps regain, balance in her life. We don't have to be a millionaire to make these choices. Some of the most generous and well-balanced individuals that are living today are living a life that society deems to be in the poverty level. It does not matter what we have, if we are coming from a place of holding onto whatever it is that we have and being stingy with it, we are being thrown into a life that is out of balance. A winner by society's definition can quickly become a loser if life is out of balance. This is why we see those who have been deemed to have it all (like those afore-mentioned singers and actors) live a life where their demons chase them in a public forum. They are drastically out of balance and do not even realize it because they are so far out of tune with their own internal needs.

It is usually easier to notice the body and mind components when we are out of balance but it is much more difficult to recognize spiritual needs and much more difficult yet to know what we need to do to bring the spiritual aspect of ourselves back into balance. There is nothing wrong with wanting to see ourselves in the winner's circle. What we need to realize when we are discussing this topic is that we are already in that circle. Because we are here, on this planet, in this body, in this time-space continuum, we are already winners. There is no one anywhere on this planet that is capable of contributing what we can contribute. We are one of a kind. If that makes you feel insignificant, it should do just the opposite. You are not unimportant, you are indeed very important. Without your contribution, and your association with others, they could not become who they are destined to become. Instead of feeling great, we look in the mirror and determine that our hair looks so bad that we are just going to stay at home, we do not want to be seen because our body is not to our liking, and we avoid interacting with others because we think we are insignificant. Nothing can be further from the truth, and until we accept this truth about ourselves and internalize it, we are allowing ourselves to be kept out of balance!

If this is true, then why in the world do we not feel like the winners that we are? It is because we are listening to other people tell us that we are not. We are listening to the ad campaigns whose job it is to convince us that we are imperfect. They need to convince us of our imperfection so that we will buy their product. We are watching models whose pictures have been photographically altered to this society's idea of perfection and basing our value of our body on something that is not real. Why is it that we have decided that someone we don't even know is better at judging us then we are of judging ourselves? It is only because we have been receiving messages through the years that we are choosing to believe rather than that little voice within us that is screaming to get out, to be free, and to enjoy life. When you look at your life, the ups and the downs, and realize that no matter where you are, you are exactly who you are and where you need to be at this time and place. You will be on your way to gaining balance when this concept becomes a part of you. If you like what you see, then keep doing what you are doing. If you do not like what you see, then begin getting yourself ready for the ride of your life, the ride that will get you to that place you, yourself, want to be. Get there for YOU! Do not get there for your spouse, or your parent, or your best friend, or your children. Get there because you cannot imagine a life where you are not already there!

When we step back and evaluate ourselves and our lives we know this to be true. It is when we base our worth on what society, media, and the opinions of others are trying to tell us that we become insecure about our own worth. It is when we begin to live our life authentically, with our own desires and positive traits shining through to others that we begin on the road to our best self.

In my first book, "Embracing Your Best Self," I shared my journey and how I got there. I wrote it in an effort to organize all of the different information I was absorbing myself. Because I had achieved such a phenomenal shift in my own personal life and views, I felt that to publish it and share it might help others. Those who have read it and talked to me about it felt that it caused them to think about some of the things in their life a bit differently. My path is mine alone, but in acknowledging that, I also realize that there are others on that path with me for a portion of time. They may be there for a short time only or they may be there with me for a considerable time. It does not matter, because their steps are not taken in exactly the same way. We are therefore on parallel paths. In my journey, I find that I am on a solitary path, and that is okay because it gives me time to assess different parts of the journey. Other times I appreciate when I find those who are on a similar path so that viewpoints can be shared. It has been along this recent leg of my journey that I have realized my importance in the entire tapestry of life. I have come to appreciate my contribution to others' paths. I have begun to see that regardless of the observable parts of my life, there is more to me than what can be seen and heard, indeed my essence is what is significant. It is when we recognize, realize, and accept our essential significance to the lives around us that we can realize that we are winners.

When we consider winning and losing, we are once again a product of our environment, our personality type, and our view of what winning and losing actually is. If, in my case, I were to consider what I would think I needed to do to "win" in a 5K run, I would only need to show up and participate. The very act of committing to take part in the race would make me feel like a winner. Do I feel like a loser because I have never run in a 5K race? Not at all, because this activity holds no value to me, and therefore I am not thrown out of balance by my inaction. If I were to decide that I wanted to participate in a 5K run and consistently made excuses as to why I could not participate, I would be throwing myself out of balance.

When we are working on balancing our life, we have to realize that each of us find balance in different ways by different things. What is winning behavior for some is not for others and the same can be said of losing behavior. One extremely important concept that we cannot discount is that we each have behaviors, actions, and activities that strike a chord within us that call our attention to feeling like a winner or a loser. We often do not have a clue about some of the struggles that others are experiencing. When we make an assumption about the actions and abilities of others we can very quickly throw ourselves off balance. If a person is extremely athletic, fit, and competitive, they will view a 5K run much differently than someone who is using the experience as a social activity. Just as we will admit that we cannot judge a book by its cover, we have to realize that we cannot judge a "winner" or a "loser" by one activity and one observation of that activity.

Another contributing factor in the winner/loser conundrum is that we each not only have our view of what winning and losing means in a certain activity, but also what priority do we place on winning and losing as it relates to the balancing of our best self.

I AM WHAT I THINK I AM

We are exactly who we think we are. There are parts of me that have not aged significantly in the last thirty years. I was discussing aging with my thirty-eight year old son not long ago. There are aspects of aging that I am not enamored with, and it was some of those aspects that I was discussing with him. I shrugged, and said, "I just have to accept that I am no longer thirty-five." He looked at me as he chuckled and said, "Mom, I am no longer thirty –five either." I then, very blithely said, "Yes, but you are still young. It isn't as important." As I have reflected on that conversation, I realized that it doesn't matter where we are, we are no longer somewhere else. Once we leave a time and space where we are, we are indeed, elsewhere. The admonitions of teachers like Eckhart Tolle become much more important as we are encouraged to live in the "now" of our lives.

While the revolutions around the sun may continue to add up, our lives are what we make of them. I saw recently on Facebook that sixty is now considered to be middle aged, rather than the forty that was accepted only a few years ago. Once again, as I consider where I am in the aging process, who do I listen to? Do I follow the actuarial tables used by the insurance companies? Or, perhaps, I let myself be influenced by all of the mailings of AARP. When I do not allow my chronological age to dominate my thoughts but allow each day to be the best it can be, I am becoming more balanced and I am enjoying my life more.

One of the most exhilarating moments in my life happened during a PBS show hosted by Dr. Wayne Dyer a few years ago when his book, "Wishes Fulfilled" was published. He had a series of photos of himself from baby on throughout his life until the present. He stated that we are not our bodies. Because I have always had such a difficult time with body image and identification with my body, this was extremely freeing. We are not our bodies. Our physical body exists for many reasons, but it does not exist to give us our identity. Our identity comes from something more ethereal than a physical pod. When we take charge of our thoughts and either allow or dismiss them as our truths, we can gain balance. Do I always follow this bit of information? No, sadly I listen too often to the fashion magazines telling me that I am imperfect, that I need to lose weight, that I am too large to be attractive, and that my value is diminished because of my body's size. I listen and sometimes I hold those thoughts longer than I need to. Other times, I shrug them off and allow my beauty and my magnificence to shine through. When I listen to my inner voice rather than those messages, I regain my balance.

We will never be able to control those sixty thousand or so thoughts running through our minds. There is no way we can do that. What we can do is slow down those thoughts, become conscious and aware of what messages those thoughts are giving us, and reclaim our ability to choose which thoughts and messages we accept for our truth. It is in this vein that we become what we think we are. If we believe we are unattractive, we will feel unattractive and we will reflect that back to those who view us. You can look around anywhere and you can see those people who feel unattractive from within and those who feel attractive. It has nothing to do with looks, but rather how they feel. I have seen some people who are very nice looking, but they choose hairstyles and clothes that indicate they do not think that they are pretty. Look at any of the "makeover" shows that Oprah sometimes has and you can see the difference. One or two insignificant things like a haircut or a choice of clothing can bring out the inner goddess in a person. Not one thing about that person has changed other than how they are thinking about themselves. It shows through and because their thoughts about themselves have changed, they have truly changed who they now think they are.

When I was in the field of education, I saw this time and time again. When students are introduced to material that they cannot understand, they feel that they are not capable of understanding, ever. That is not so. You only have to look around at the capabilities of our youth today compared to what was expected fifty years ago (in my case) and see that they are very capable. That is not to say that they are capable in the traditional sense of education, but they are capable. It reminds me that Thomas Edison was sent home at a young age and his mother was told that he was slow and incapable of being taught anything. He is one of the most prolific and well-known inventors of any era. Everyone has the ability to learn. We learn at different rates, in different ways, and for different reasons. Many people think that if a person has a college degree it is because they are smart. A college degree means that a person successfully completed the classes necessary to gain that degree. It has as much to do with intent and focus as it does innate ability. We are a product of our thoughts, and to go one step further, we are a product of the thoughts we choose to accept and make our truth.

I recently spoke with a friend about an inspirational program she was fortunate enough to see. There was a program offered by one of the quilting guilds with a blind quilter. Yes, a blind quilter. She shared with me the inspiration offered by a woman who had been in a horrific automobile accident in her early thirties and became blind as a result of her injuries. The program was at times humorous and at times extremely emotional. What message everyone left with was this: If a blind woman can quilt, you can do anything you decide to do! What a powerful message for us all. We can do what we think we can do. If we make a decision about our life we will find a way around any obstacle placed in our path that may attempt to keep us from that desire. We are who we think we are. We look at some of those people who serve as inspirations to us and admire the struggle they overcame not realizing that the power they possessed in that achievement, we also possess.

We are inundated with so much information in this technological age. Social media has become, for me, the doorway to a greater amount of information than I would ever have imagined. We are free, as with any information we get, to accept or reject any of the information we choose. Much of what is shared on social media is not really fact, but rather opinion touted as fact. One has to be aware of this and filter closely whether we are going to accept something as fact. When I receive inspirational posts, it is not necessary to use that filter because inspiration comes from a variety of sources and reflects a spiritual need rather than a sharing of information. It is when we share those spiritual ponderings that we are able to take what our own spirit needs and absorb it to help us achieve a balance in our lives. If we are profoundly touched, we can choose to share those items that have touched our psyche with others so that their spirit, too, can be touched.

Much of our inspirational sharing, whether in social media or other venues, serves to help us keep a balance in our own physicality. Inspiration can come from written words, beauty of nature, art, music, dance, etc. It comes from everywhere and comes at us from every direction. I can be inspired to be a better parent when I see how others interact with their children. We can inspire by example. It is when we express our best selves that we inspire others to express their best selves. When we come from a place that is balanced we are more able to achieve that best self and that best life. When that happens, our very lives are an inspiration to others. When we realize that we are capable of this kind of inspiration, it inspires us even further, and the circle keeps on going. What we often find is that we can get bogged down by thinking we are less than we are and that we are no longer capable of being the best we can be. We know what we want, but suddenly insecurities invade, and we think of ourselves as imperfect. Well, we are all imperfect and that is exactly okay. We are not living this life to strive for perfection, yet it is that very idea of perfection that is often our biggest stumbling block to a magnificent life. We very often accept mediocrity in our life and shrug off becoming our best selves simply because we are afraid. There is a Marianne Williamson quote that basically says that what scares us the most is not fear of failure, but the fear of our magnificence, and I think that is true. When we are living our lives at full throttle and achieving our desires, we are scared of our innate power. In order to achieve balance when we are at this stage, it only requires us to form a commitment with ourselves.

MAKE A COMMITMENT TO YOURSELF

If you are going to live a balanced life there are several things that you will have to admit, understand, and act upon. Much of the time we simply have no clue where we are truly headed and what path we need to take to get there. All we sometimes hold onto is where we want to end up. We don't concentrate on where we are but rather become consumed with where we will be in the future and how much more fulfilled we will be then. This is commonly referred to as "destination obsession" a phenomenon that plagues us all in one way or another at some times. We anticipate the vacation rather than enjoy brief periods of peace and quiet as they are presented daily. We think of the satisfaction that some future event will bring us and as a result become disappointed with what we're currently experiencing in life.

With the laws that control the universe, such as the Law of Attraction, how we feel about our life in the present is of the utmost importance.   All that we are is energy vibrating at different frequencies. The objects we view and think are solid are actually only solid because of the vibrational frequency they are emitting. There is more space between particles than there are particles of matter. This is an extremely difficult concept to wrap our minds around because, after all, we can reach out and touch that solid object. If we are going to live that balanced life and achieve our desires, we need to be certain of what it is that we actually want. Too often we express a desire, but what we are expressing is not what we actually want. We think that when we reach a certain weight or have a certain job or home that our life will be better. We do not allow ourselves to be content with what we are and what we have at this point. It is when we realize that all we have is now and that every moment is actually now that we are free to experience each "now" moment exactly as we please. When we live our lives totally in the "now," we will have the life we wish to have.

In order for this appreciation to work in our lives, we need to take the time and effort to contemplate exactly what it is that we desire our life to be. Until we do this, it is rather like deciding to take a trip and not consulting a road map in order to get from here to our destination. We need to be aware of not only the direction we are going but also the roads that we will take to get there. Once we have done the planning we are free to enjoy the trip each mile at a time. It is this way in our lives also. While we do not want to be consumed by where we will end up, we want to at least have some idea of where we are headed. If we want a job but make no effort to search job openings and send in applications, it is highly unlikely that we will get the job of our dreams. The idea is to ask, realize that the Universe is scrambling to help us get there, and place ourselves in the position to allow for what we have asked to come into our lives. In order to do this, we need to make some commitments. Commitments to ourselves, commitments to our journey, and commitments to creating an atmosphere of undeniable faith that will ensure that what we want will come to us.

In making commitments, we will experience more success when we more clearly we express our desires. The more specifically we express our hopes and dreams, the sooner and more easily they can be achieved. What happens so often is that if we express a desire and it does not come to us in the or at the time that we had hoped for we become discouraged and give up on that desire. When we give up we then set ourselves up for keeping that desire away from manifestation. It is difficult for us deal with some of the disappointments in life unless we see that it is only when our thoughts are adjusted and we put ourselves in alignment to the vibrations of our desires that we will achieve them. When we keep ourselves in a constant state of gratitude for all that we currently have we are in alignment with our wishes and desires.

How we do this may vary from individual to individual, but the process is really the same. We do this by placing our internal vibrations in the highest alignment. Then, we will be in a state of allowing what we want in our lives. This is the commitment we need to make, and there is homework involved to get us to this point of allowing. It does not matter what goal we are seeking. When we put ourselves in that place of true love and appreciation for all that is already ours, then we are in that place that will allow our desires to come to us. Making ourselves available for our desires is the ultimate commitment we need to make. We can first list and be very specific about what we want and then we can go to that place of joy and happiness knowing that it is on its way. The only reason that more of us do not see our dreams manifested more often is that we have been conditioned to think that we need to do something or to be something in order for our dreams to come to us. We think that we need to work harder or be more beautiful or be smarter or be something that we are not in order to deserve something better. That is simply our ego getting in our way. We are already deserving and we are already good enough. Once we realize this, it will happen. Our listing and narrowing down homework allows us to concentrate on the affirmative and positive vibrations that focusing on those desires can bring to us. We begin thinking in terms of already being in possession of our dreams, and our vibrations begin to align with those dreams. This is the magic of life itself showing up in our reality.

When we put something down on paper, we instantly solidify it in our minds. That is the reason that many people write their affirmations down in addition to repeating them. While I have never consistently kept a journal, it is when I write down my thoughts and desires on a somewhat regular basis that I find I have the best success in directing good experiences to my life. The more concise we are with our desires, the more easily we see results. We cannot repeatedly say one thing and behave in a way that is diametrically opposed to that. One of two things will happen: we will either realize that what we are saying we want we do not actually want, or we get our behavior in alignment with that desire and behave in a way that will line us up for allowing it to come to us. This is the only way that the Universe operates. It is only when we commit to ourselves that we begin to see results. Anything less than a full commitment is simply wishful thinking and pie-in-the-sky day dreaming. Take time now and begin this part of your journey by truly deciding what it is you wish to manifest and committing your direction to achieving these desires. Write them down, be precise, and refer to them many times a day until you have totally aligned with these desires.

Once you have made the decisions and adjustments to your thinking that will help you achieve your desires, there is one other point that is crucial to the achievement of those desires. You must simply quit thinking about the how and the why and live your life in that place of already having achievement in your life. Until you can do this, you will find yourself in a state of turmoil and concern about when or how something will happen. Let's consider the example of abundance. Let us say that you have expressed a desire for a certain amount of money or a certain expensive object in your life, and you have it in your mind very specifically. You must then turn your attention away from the achievement. You must focus on the fact that receiving it is a "done deal." When you begin to be concerned that the money is not there, you are focusing on that "not having" rather than the "having" and you are pushing achievement further and further away from becoming a reality. Getting the desire into focus is necessary, but to continue to focus on the "not already there" is going to be counterproductive. Because it did not come on your time schedule in your imagined way, you are in essence throwing out the baby with the bathwater. You feel that the Universe is conspiring against you. What is happening is that you are not taking the time, effort, and commitment to yourself to get in alignment with your desires.

PART TWO

MAKING COMMITMENTS THAT WILL KEEP YOU IN BALANCE

This portion of the book will reflect an actual look into my life, what my imbalances are, and how I intend to get my balance back. I will set my intent and direct my vibrations to align with those intentions. I will share the daily corrections that I make in order to keep those intentions on course. At the end of ninety days I will share how closely my desires are aligning with my best self. At that point, you will be able to see how you can take the imbalances in your life and align your desires and your intentions with a ninety day commitment to get closer to the life you want to lead. You cannot jump from being totally out of alignment into perfect alignment without effort. The closer you are to serving your best self, the less time you will require for coming into balance. Given these constructs, let the challenge begin.

While we concern ourselves with the mind/body/spirit balance, we come to realize that our environment plays a factor in the balance of our lives also. We have wishes and desires that are dependent upon that environment to some extent. I look critically, yet kindly, at how my life is evolving. I find much satisfaction in it for the most part. I do however see that

I currently am allowing myself the freedom of procrastination. Procrastination, or that fine art of postponing doing something that we feel the necessity of doing, can become a tremendous factor in throwing us off balance. I had always hoped for the time in life where I could indulge my love of reading. I now have that time and in the indulgence of my desire to read, I have inadvertently thrown my life out of balance by removing a focus on anything other than reading. I realize that I have allowed that love to override a desire for a well-cared-for home and garden. I have indulged myself to the point that I am putting off every daily task as long as possible so that I can continue to read.

My first step will be to evaluate both the inside and outside of my home and work out a plan that will show results in ninety days. It will include the amount of time that I am willing to commit to each area. I am not going to anticipate the end result. I am planning for a balance, not an outcome. Too often we jump ahead to the outcome of any of our desires and lose ourselves in the how and when part of the equation. When we take the how and when out, we can focus our attention in a relaxed manner, knowing that the balance will occur. This experiment is beginning during last week of April so it will end during the last week of July.

It is interesting that the more we have to do, the more we usually get done. When we are younger and have families and jobs to juggle in addition to household chores and social obligations, we seem to organize our time better and place our priorities where they need to be. Since I have retired, I have accomplished much that has required blocks of time, but I have noticed that I also can put off those chores that I am not particularly fond of. I didn't have that luxury thirty-five years ago. While the idea of balancing ourselves is to give our lives more ease and enjoyment in the moment, we have to commit to those chores we are not so very fond of, whatever they may be.

My list is rather lengthy but I think by asking these relevant questions, we can each begin to regain our balance. Keep in mind that as long as you are working in the direction you want to go, you are regaining balance. You will achieve balance to some degree each time you have kept a commitment to yourself, regardless of the scope of that commitment. Also know that what keeps you out of balance may mean nothing to someone else. What you will see that is throwing me out of balance may cause you no difficulty whatsoever. **It is not the issue itself that is causing us to be out of balance, but rather the lack of attention to any issue that causes us a degree of angst or displeasure. It is when we do not attend to those issues in a timely fashion that we become imbalanced.** The longer this imbalance is allowed to remain, the more imbalanced we become and as we become more imbalanced, we operate at lower and lower vibrations and lose much of the higher vibrations that are needed if we want to live a life as our best self. Ready to get started? Let's go for it!!

DAY ONE - WORKSHEET: AREAS OF MY LIFE THAT REQUIRE FURTHER SCRUTINY

1. What jobs am I avoiding in my own home? Am I avoiding them because I will need help accomplishing them, or because I don't want to do them? How much time am I willing to spend on a daily or weekly basis to address these problems? Can I find ways to take larger jobs and compartmentalize them so that they can be more easily tackled? What do I need to do in order to make a positive change and where am I willing to begin?

Jobs that I am avoiding:

1. Thorough cleaning and decluttering of unneeded items. – I need to thoroughly clean all of the rooms in my home. I also need to address closets and drawers and storage areas and get rid of items that I no longer love or use. I will need help in doing this in order to keep me going forward. I am willing to find someone who can help me clean and organize on a regular basis, and I am willing to tackle some of the decluttering chores for a minimum of fifteen minutes per day, seven days a week until I am satisfied* with the results and there is no longer a feeling of being overwhelmed. I know that when I am overwhelmed, I am very much out of balance.

(* We are free to decide our own level of satisfaction. If, for example I have certain areas in my garage that I want to de-clutter and other areas that are okay, as is, then those areas that are okay are not affecting my balance and I do not have to do anything in those areas. I may, however, find that after I have corrected those areas that are causing me problems I am more than willing to go ahead with other areas. The choices are ours and ours alone when we are working on balancing ourselves. We can only do what we need to do. This is so often why there is discord in families. Areas that create imbalance for one do not create imbalance for others. If you try to get others to buy into your imbalance by thinking that they are ever going to see the importance of something like "putting towels in a hamper", then you are asking for a greater degree of imbalance. It happens, and in order for us to regain our balance, we must be aware of this and we must learn to deal with it in a way that creates our own peace. Dealing with it may mean ignoring what annoys you and "put the towels in the hamper" yourself. The goal is to create your own balance and thus your own happiness, and not rely on the actions of others to do it for you.)

2. Are there long term jobs inside my home that will require me to find workers for them and will require a budget or savings to accomplish them? Can I prioritize any of these jobs? Do I have a time frame or are these just desired achievements that have nothing to do with my balance but rather they are things which I will find aesthetically pleasing?

I have lived in my home for over five years and when I moved here, I got rid of a great deal of "stuff." I decided that I would not bring anything new into my house unless I first got rid of two items. I have honored that fairly well, but I am finding that I never really made this house my own. I would like to thoroughly assess the desirability of the furnishings I now have and get rid of those that no longer reflect my taste and my life as it is now. If I do this cleansing, I will be making room for new items that will need to be budgeted for. There is not a time frame for this. I will need help in accomplishing these changes because while I like a beautiful home, I do not enjoy the shopping that is necessary to find those items that appeal to me. I have made a decision to contact a design studio and work with them to get my house to become the home that will allow me to create in the way that gives me the highest degree of balance and happiness.

3. Are there areas in my yard and garden that need my attention to regain balance? What jobs am I avoiding in my yard and garden? Are those areas that I can do myself or will I need to have help? What amount of time am I willing to commit to spending on getting my yard and garden to an acceptable state that will help me regain my balance and thus regain my best self? When and where will I commit to beginning this effort?

I enjoy my yard but I find that I am enjoying the work that it takes to keep it looking nice less and less each year. Five years ago I started the flower beds that are now there. I have added to them each year but none of them are completely finished. I am going to look for someone to help me in the yard on a regular basis in order to keep these areas weeded and mulched. I am willing to commit to a minimum of thirty minutes every day that is available to work in the yard. If it is not raining or has not rained in twenty-four hours, I will deem that to be an appropriate day for yard work. It will be my goal to finalize two areas in the backyard as well as the area along the fence and the area in front of the patio in the front yard.

4. Are there any long-term items in the yard or garden that cause me to take my focus away from my best self and cause me to be disrupted and irritated?

In my case, I cannot see anything other than just general gardening chores. There is no outside maintenance to my house or my yard that requires hiring outside workers and an outlay of money.

5. Are there other areas in my environment – outside my physical mind/body/ spirit – that I am avoiding dealing with? What are those areas and what can I do to improve those areas and get back into balance?

I do not have other concerns that I am aware of that are keeping me out of balance. Since I can think of none, that means that for me, there are none. [For some of you there might be issues with a car, a job, or something else that may be disrupting your life that is in the environment rather than the specific mind/body/spirit balance.]

REVIEW: I have determined that my procrastination has led me to a cluttered and disorganized home. I have established some short term and long term goals that will help me regain a balanced calm in my life so that I am functioning at a higher vibration. I also have some issues with procrastination in my garden, and they need to be addressed as well. In both cases, I will require extra help, at least temporarily, to get these areas back in order.

DAY TWO – GETTING STARTED, HOW DID IT GO?

On day two I have enlisted the help of a young woman, Kathy, who I found to help me clean. We reviewed what results I want to see, and I informed her that I had no time frame. I need a thorough cleaning and I will need her help with organization and decluttering. We got to know each other and began on thoroughly cleaning the bathrooms and washing the kitchen floor. We established her next visit, and I feel much more dedicated to finishing what has now been started. As for the yard work, it was a cool rainy day and I did not get to those tasks.

I began thinking about the mind/body/spirit balance and without setting down for the questions I need to ask, I realize that I am going to need to work on the body aspect of this triad in order to regain my overall balance. I do not have overriding thoughts of imbalance when I consider the mind or the spirit in this group, therefore, for me, mind and spirit are in balance. Because I spend an inordinate amount of time focusing on the body I don't have, I am not allowing my body to operate at its maximum efficiency. Because my focus is on what I do not have, the Universe is delivering that to me. Keep in mind as we continue our journey that the Universe is only inclusive. We are used to saying, "no, I do not want that." The universe hears, "give me that which I do not want," and we continue to be kept from what we think we are asking for. It may sound confusing, but just remember..... If you are focusing on what you already have, you will continue to get just what you are getting. When you shift your focus and your thoughts to a life that already has this in reality, the universe will give you the object of your focus.

As I go into Day 3, I need to remember that I will be asking myself what it is that I can truly commit to. I do not have to commit to everything at once because I can increase my commitment as I go along. The goal is to honor the journey to the goal knowing that we never get there because when we get to where we want to be, there will always be new desires.

DAY THREE –

Today my daughter-in-law was able to come and help me for about four hours. I decided that it would be good to begin working on clearing out four pieces of furniture that I was going to get rid of. They no longer go with the design of my current home, and they are large bulky pieces that really don't fit within the feel of the house. When I began in the spare room, I opened up the cedar chest and as I moved it out, there was a dampness and mildew on the baseboard, and the veneer on the chest was coming off on one end. I had only planned on moving this to another room, but decided rather than make repairs, I will just pass it on to someone who would like to rework it. We unloaded quilts from this piece and an armoire in another room and made a pile for me to keep, a pile for my daughter and granddaughter, a pile for my son, daughter-in-law and grandsons, and a pile that I can either sell or give away. All of the forty-plus quilts will need to be washed so that will be my task over the next several days. In this volume of stored quilts there were table toppers, wall hangings, and other small quilts to find homes for. We also began clearing some drawers that had fabric and patterns for projects that I had hoped to do at one time. I was as ruthless as I could be in giving critical thought to what I would actually do, and in the process, I created a small shopping bag of patterns that I will share with some friends who quilt. What they will use, they can have and if there are patterns left, they can take them to their quilt guild. While this activity created work, it was a great start to my decluttering process. The weather was still cool and rainy today, so my yard commitment has been put on hold, as agreed.

While this kind of self-talk may seem unnecessary, it can give you a dialogue with yourself that can help keep you on track and focused on the progress rather than any lack of progress. You may choose to journal, like I am doing here, or you can get a daily desk calendar and list your accomplishments by the hour. Perhaps you have a bulletin board and want to keep track on that. The choices are yours, and you will need to pick something that you are comfortable with. If I did not choose to share my progress with you, I would probably use an hourly desk calendar book and record that way. I chose to share simply because when we are transparent in our attempts, we cannot shirk our commitment. I cannot make it up or there will be nothing accomplished in the next ninety days. Always remember that those ninety days will pass whether we do anything or not to create our path back to balance in our lives or not.

The longer we are in balance, the sooner we recognize an imbalance and the sooner we can make small adjustments to regain balance. I allowed external circumstances to draw my thoughts away from a balanced focus and in the process created my imbalance. Just three days into this process, I am already beginning to feel the difference that taking action is making in my life.

DAY FOUR THROUGH SEVEN

I am into this commitment for a week. I can feel that I am settling in and have been keeping the commitments to myself. I have had some help getting started and that is pulling me back into balance. I am seeing that my goals can be achieved if I am willing to do two things: I will need to be persistent, and I will need to be patient. Patience is something that many people find very difficult to achieve. It requires a great deal of faith in ourselves and our ability to endure what we need to in order to see our desires come to fruition. We want the results and we want them now. It is when we fall back on the teachings of Eckhart Tolle and others that help us. We can become patient when we accept the waiting as part of the achieving. When we embrace the waiting as fully as we embrace the results, we will become patient. I used to get extremely anxious when I was traveling anywhere, whether it was across town or across the country, and encountered road construction. I was impatient, and that impatience led to anxiety because there was something blocking me from getting on to my destination. As I learned about the power of now, and embraced those times of slowing down, I was able to enjoy them. I could observe different kinds of vehicles, I could appreciate the scenery more fully, and I could take a bit of a break from the pressure of driving non-stop. I realized that it was extremely important in my journey for the slowing to take place. It was in that brief stopping that I was getting where I was supposed to get exactly when I was to get there. If I had not been stopped, I might have arrived at the wrong time for the events I was needed to participate in. It is that way with any event in which we become impatient, the delay in achieving the goal is important in a way we may never be cognizant of, but it is important. Honor those delays.

As I continue de- cluttering, I can see that I am engaging in a sharing time. I am letting go of items that no longer serve me and am allowing those items to serve others. I have discovered a renewal of interest in some of my creative endeavors and have an opportunity for an outlet in which I can share my talents with others. As I have found some help, I have expanded my circle of friends, and I am getting information on others who can help me reach my goals both inside and outside of my house.

Because I have made a commitment to both this book and my previous book, because I made a commitment to my environment and soon my physical body, I had to turn down an opportunity to spend a month in England. It is not my time to go back to England, but the windows to that opportunity are still open, and this adventure will be added to the list of desires which is necessary for all of us. In the search for balance, we need to be aware that a constant addition and subtraction of desires is going to happen. It is when we commit to a desire that we put ourselves on the pathway to achieving it. We have really what we can think of as three kinds of desires: passing desires, lukewarm desires, and burning (GOTTA DO IT!) desires. The passing desires are those that we give brief consideration to. They may be as simple as a passing desire to think about what kind of tattoo we would get if we were so inclined to a passing desire to take a trip to Bora Bora. It is a brief thought with maybe some daydreaming involved, but it is never a true desire that we take seriously. Then there are the lukewarm desires, these are desires that return from time to time. We may think of a particular career, but we don't make any steps to getting the education needed to have that career. It is the kind of desire that we call pipe dreams. We think about them, but that is all we do, think. Then there are those desires that don't let go of us. They are the desires we cannot shake. They become a part of us, and it is when we focus on those that we learn to think in a way that we will make those desires a part of our lives.

A balanced life will contain all three of those kinds of desires, as it should. We can sometimes take a lukewarm desire and it can become a burning desire, and vice versa. Our desires change, and if we are in balance, we allow this flow without question and without stress. We need to realize when we have a burning desire, we may be just a hair away from achieving it when we decide to give up on it. It is when we decide that we will never give up on a desire that we are aiming our intent and our focus on that desire. When we give this focus, it will be achieved. We are placing ourselves in a vibrational pattern that will allow those desires to come into our lives. Balance is achieved.

DAY EIGHT THROUGH FOURTEEN - The differences that a week can make when we are intent upon achieving a goal is interesting and came from a totally surprising place. It has been during this time that Vanity Fair issued a story about the former Olympic athlete, Bruce Jenner, and his transition to Caitlyn Jenner. When we are talking about balancing our lives, it is very easy for us to become focused on our own balance. This is as it should be. We need to also realize, as I have come to realize this week, that in our personal balancing, we cannot overlook our need to come into balance with our views on societal issues. In the case of Bruce/Caitlyn Jenner, I find that I am currently allowing the opinions of others throw me off balance. This is a real story about a male Olympic athlete who won a gold medal in the 1976 Olympic Games. It is also a story of a man who realized at some point during his life that there was the soul and spirit of a woman who had come to this incarnation in a man's body. It is the story of a courageous sixty-five year old woman who braved speculation and public ridicule to free her true self from the prison that a male body provided for so many years. This man had helped raise ten children, six of which were his biological children. This woman chose to free herself to live her life as she felt she was truly meant to be. This story has created all sorts of news and conflict from people who are, in reality, unimportant in the whole grand scheme of things, including me. It is a story, however, that I cannot seem to let go of. It is a story that brings to my mind what I feel one of the important issues is, and it is one that the public will not consider. In the freeing of herself, what impact is being made on her heirs? None of the decisions we make in life is a static decision. All of our decisions are like the proverbial pebble dropped into the water with the ensuing ripples.

There have been many very negative unkind comments about Jenner's transformation. That does not throw me off balance. I have dealt with the demons in my own life that led me to assume that everyone was on the same page that I was on. I have accepted that we all have a path, they are all different, and one person's path is not better or worse than ours. All of the paths are needed to create the tapestry that is our life. What I find amazing is that in these comments we are calling into usage the words "hero" and "courage." When we use those words they bring forth, evidently, all sorts of issues for many people. When I was young, my heroes were the Lone Ranger and Tonto, Hopalong Cassidy, and The Cisco Kid. Then in my early teens it was President Kennedy. As an adult in my thirties it was, and still is former President, Jimmy Carter, and his wife, Rosalynn. Now in my sixties, I have added young men and women who are stretching the limits of what society has formerly deemed acceptable and they are making the people in this world much more aware of accepting and celebrating differences. Young women like Malala Yousafzai cause us to look at our lives and hopefully become more compassionate, loving, and embracing because of the ideals that they have fought for and brought to the forefront.

Right now, the above mentioned Bruce Jenner has transitioned into a woman named Caitlyn Jenner. He is being deemed a hero, and there are many people posting pictures of those individuals that they think are heroes. What they are forgetting is that we are all heroes to someone. I will repeat that..... **We are all heroes to someone.** A former student posted this on Facebook and I think it is worthy of a share:

> "I have read all day about how Caitlyn Jenner is not a hero. She isn't a hero in the typical sense of the word. She didn't fight alongside the brave men and women that fight for our country. She didn't struggle everyday with cancer as she continued her love of the game. Maybe she isn't YOUR hero. She is, however someone's. To all the people struggling with their identity, to all the people who are afraid to be who they are, to all the people that struggle to live a life uncomfortable in their own skin, to all the people who didn't think they were 'appropriate,' to live this life, she is a hero. This life is full of discrimination and hatred to all those who are different. To those struggling, Caitlyn has shown them that it's okay to decide what is right for you, no matter what scrutiny you face. She has decided to embrace her struggles, made some

serious adjustments in her appearance, she should be deemed a hero. A hero to all those that struggle with transgender, or whatever else is holding them back from finding their true happy. I applaud you and for the many lives that finally find smiles and acceptance, I thank you. May this new journey find the rest of her days in peace and in total happiness?"

Another former student addressed the concept of courage in this way:

"Celebrating one person's courage doesn't take away from the courage of another. There is enough celebration to go around." I think she nailed it right on the head. There are many different kinds of situations that are courageous. It is courageous when a person joins the armed forces and leaves their family and friends to serve our country. It is courageous when a baby lets go of any support and takes their first step. It takes courage for a doctor to face the family of a dying patient. It also takes courage for a famous male Olympic athlete to decide at sixty-five to take a step into who he has known he is for most of his life. Anyone who takes a step into the unknown is exhibiting courage, and we all do that in some way. When we expand our definition of "hero" and "courage" we are able to look at those who judge with more compassion. When we view with compassion, we are getting ourselves back into balance.

The above paragraphs represent an example of how one can take a journal and use that to get back into balance. I was very off kilter until I let it all process onto paper. I was able to look at the issue and separate myself enough to become more neutral so that I could view it in a way that would encourage rather than discourage my balance. I am very thankful that the only "news" that I have received has been over Facebook because I can only imagine how the emergence of Caitlyn Jenner has been on television. I, personally, think that she was very courageous, and I think that she will contribute greatly to our understanding of the transgender community.

Once we have an idea about who we really are, the "me" behind all of the egoic self, we are free to act upon it. At the beginning, like with most new things that are introduced into our life, we are seduced into thinking that the newness will last. It doesn't. As the euphoric high of discovering and embracing our best selves wears off, we then begin to confront the issues we always had to confront. We do not live in a vacuum. What we begin to realize is that we confront the issues differently and they are truly more easily addressed than they were before we became enlightened. After confronting the ups and downs in our life we come to realize that the answer to making a more peaceful and contented life for ourselves lies in the idea of balancing our ups and downs. When we strive to keep most of the issues in our life on a steady course, we are more easily able to deal with the sharp ups and downs that come our way. We no longer linger in the low areas, and we hold the highs in greater esteem and thus allow them to last longer. The result is a well-balanced life that can weather those times of turmoil in society that we once thought were so very important.

We get issues coming into our lives on a daily basis. What causes anxiety in one person does not cause anxiety in another. Regardless of what we think about it is important to remember that we are in charge of the thoughts that stay with us and the ones that we release. Consciously balancing our thoughts and retaining those that give us a greater degree of what can only be termed "feel good" thoughts is the one most important bit of information you can receive. It is when we only allow those thoughts that are surrounded with love, appreciation, and joy that we create a life reflective of those feelings.

DAY FIFTEEN THROUGH TWENTY-TWO

As I find my commitment to my home and garden coming into focus, I am beginning to want to work on the body connection to getting myself back into balance. In order to do this, I have to look at not only my desire but my willingness to commit to a healthier way of life. If I choose to look at how I eat and exercise as a chore or a way of denying myself, I realize that I will never achieve permanent success. I am beginning to look at a deeper desire. I begin to see the great gift of a healthier and more supple body as a true gift to the inner goddess that is me. When I see it as a celebration rather than a denial, I can come more easily into balance. This is not to say that this conversion of thought will be an easy one, but it is not to say that it will be that difficult either. It will be a different way of thinking about food. In this seven days, I am going to assess my body's needs from a place of actual nutrients rather than focusing on an emotional attachment to certain foods. I have used food as a panacea for what I have thought of as lack, usually lack of love. When I see that foods are here to serve our ultimate health and well-being and not as a substitute for affection, I can anticipate that the changes in my body will be phenomenal. It is an exciting time to anticipate such a gift.

This week I am finding myself inundated with nutritional information. I am looking at the ways that I have eaten food in the past that have caused me to gain weight and the way that I have used foods to help me lose weight, and I am making some discoveries that I can use to help me balance the nutritional needs of my body. I also take into account that my size is not the problem but it reflects the problem. If I am using food to fill my stomach in an effort to fill my heart, I will never, repeat, NEVER have enough. When I use food to tend to my nutritional needs and gifts from my heart to fill my heart, I will no longer have an issue with food. I can look at my current health/body/size and come up with only four things that I am needing to either eliminate or reduce in my diet. I can eliminate wheat, sugar, dairy, and reduce (with the idea of eliminating) caffeine. There are already things that I eat in limited amounts such as fats and red meat. I no longer drink sodas but I need to add more water to keep my body hydrated so that organs will function more efficiently. If I continue to add the raw foods that contain fiber, vitamins, and minerals, I will be achieving a healthier body that does not crave foods that do not contribute to my well-being.

As I implement these ways of balancing my body in the healthiest way possible, I will give myself a couple of weeks for my body to adjust. At the end of those two weeks I will need to evaluate and make any changes that I think need to be made. I am looking into adding fermented foods and doing a mild detox also.

I have, in this first three weeks, looked at the external and the internal part of the body in the mind/body/spirit connection as it reflects a balance. I will continue with the commitment I have made to myself and begin the next aspect of this dealing with the mind. I am doing this in no particular order. It was just the order that I needed to because of the needs that I perceived in my life. Your order may be different, and you may wish to read this book in its entirety to see the whole process before you embark on balancing your life. I would encourage you to take any notes of things that may cause you to think of something in your life that needs balancing. I am leaving the spiritual aspect of this triad until last because I feel that it is the area right now that needs the least amount of work, yet it will be the area that will be the best support of the other two areas and the changes being called into effect for a balance. I stress again, there is no right way or wrong way to achieve balance in your life. You may not need any major adjustments to make your life work in a way that enhances your best self, and that is really what balancing does, it takes what you have and helps create a life that is more fulfilling.

DAY TWENTY-THREE THRU THIRTY - I am going into the Memorial Day Holiday as I begin evaluating and recapping the first month of balancing. In this first month, you have seen me take three areas and make positive steps toward creating a balance. When doing this, it is critical to realize that it is never done. When you make an effort to balance, it is critical to realize that it is never done. You are actually acknowledging that an imbalance is occurring. You are then taking steps to readjust your vibrations through your actions to bring about a vibrational balance. The vibrational balance is the important balance. By this, I mean, in the case of my yard: If I could readjust my thoughts and decide that I liked the weedy jungle look, my vibrations would be adjusted. And, if that happened, then my actions would be immaterial because my vibrations would have achieved balance. In my case, I chose a different scenario. I opted to get some of the work professionally done and I will do the other, less viewed areas, at my leisure. This is how I chose to achieve balance in my life as it pertains to this aspect of my life. There is no template for balance. I am offering examples that I have chosen, but my choices and your choices will not be the same. When you are feeling great, your soul is in balance. Your body balances a bit differently, or maybe I should say, is motivated differently. Our bodies are our physical manifestation of all that we are. We come into this world at a time and in a way that we choose in order to experience what we want to experience in this incarnation.

When we are looking at a balanced life, we balance within our own set of rules. There again, my set of "rules" and your set may vary greatly. Keep in mind there is no one and only way to balance your life. You are entirely in the driver's seat when it comes to the how. I am sharing what is working for me and how I am adjusting as time goes on. We are energy, and that is all we are. What is seen and seems to be a solid (such as our physical body) is energy in motion in a way to make it appear as a solid. There is more space to our bodies than there is reality. When we are working from this assumption, we realize that what we think we can do and what we are really able to do with our lives is entirely under our control and is based on the vibrational essence of all that energy.

Before we go on to balancing the mind, I found a Reference from the Institute for the Psychology of Eating entitled "A New Definition of Metabolism," that I found to be very informative and helpful in the balance of the body. We all know that we live in a culture obsessed with perfection. Our feelings weigh down our body. The burden of not fully living can actually largely determine the shape of our bodies. Statistics show that 90% of women are dissatisfied with their bodies and 40% of girls between the ages of 9-10 have already tried to lose weight. Our body weight and shape is directly impacted by our emotional, mental, and energetic well-being. This means that who you are and how you express yourself (or don't) can significantly impact your physical form just as much as what you eat and how you exercise. On a scientific level, stress is sympathetic arousal and relaxation is parasympathetic arousal. Ideal bodily functions require that for full metabolic power to take place, the relaxation response is necessary. No matter what, if your body is chronically stressed, you will burn calories, assimilate nutrients, and digest food at an extremely reduced rate. Our external body is a reflection of our internal state. When we are not honoring who we truly are, our body receives a message that it is unsafe, wrong, or does not have permission to enter its most fully expressed and actualized form. If you are not living authentically, you create for yourself chronic stress and the effects are difficulty in losing weight, weight gain, diminished immune system, and calcium deficiency, among many other symptoms. The best things you can do is to honor yourself, trust your feelings, and express your needs and desires. Every decision you make is either supporting metabolic function or disempowering you.

DAYS THIRTY-ONE THROUGH SIXTY

During these next 4 weeks, I will continue on my current path, constantly attempting to make adjustments to my actions so that my vibrations remain as high as I can get them.

I have seen an improvement in my ability to get my vibrations in a higher frequency and I am beginning to see the manifestation of my desires in several areas. One of the most noticeable differences is the manifestation of the people I am needing to live as my best self. One notable addition is a man named Art. I had seen Art, often at Panera and we had smiled, waved, and occasionally said a few words to each other, but we had never really introduced ourselves... About one week ago, he came over and sat down and as we talked, there was a definite feeling of a previous connection. We even discussed this feeling and are pretty well convinced that we were feeling the vibrations that had been amassed over several previous lifetimes. Neither of us had ever felt anything quite so strongly upon meeting another person. During this time he found that I had written a book. He and a friend of his were discussing a novel they hoped to write, and they asked me to join in the collaboration. This was another event that added to my vibrations. I once talked to a friend about what happened when you felt that your vibrations were causing you to almost spin yourself out of the physical into pure spiritual. I think this is the feeling that I am having. We have committed to a firm friendship, and it is a time that is truly electric for me. I am writing this with such appreciation that it is difficult to even express the emotions. It is like what we observe in Disney's "Cinderella" when the Fairy Godmother waves the wand and the poorly dressed girl is changed into a beautifully dressed princess. That is the way this vibration is causing me to feel. This is where the mind aspect of our mind/body/spirit comes in.

It doesn't matter how highly we are vibrating, if we cannot hold those vibrations, we will lose some of the vibrational power. When we start using our thoughts and try to manifest anything, it is imperative that we are able to hold ourselves in vibrational alignment. It does not matter what event, action, or observation causes the alignment, it only makes a difference that it happens. The energy vibrations and friendship that Art and I are sharing has led to a creative surge. The surge, not so surprisingly, is at its peak when we are working side by side, each on our own computer. The collaboration, the ideas, and the excitement flows like a rushing stream. Like a rushing stream, the flow cannot be stopped. It can be diminished if barriers are put in its way, but the flow and the energy is always there and will always be there. This is important to accept because sparks of our own energy are left wherever we are, after we leave—we leave traces or specks of that energy, and it is there to add to the energy of someone else who encounters it.

It is at time like this when we can hold on to the vibrational alignment and not allow our egoic mental processes to override our vibrations that we can manifest glorious desires. When you get to this kind of extreme vibration there is a need created that is so strong it defies description. It is carnal and it is raw. It is the desire to become nothing but spirit. That, however, can go one way or the other, and I am going to work on this concept with you while I am in this state of alignment. We are going to explore our mind's ability to direct our energy into creative pursuits instead of floundering with destructive actions, both of which will set that spirit soaring.

When we reach that spirited vibrational alignment, we refer to that as being in the Vortex. When we are in the Vortex we are aligning ourselves with what we want to manifest. We are in a place that is beyond worrying about the when and where and how of what we want, we are spinning in the realization that all we want is there, just waiting for us to see it. To understand the mental aspect of our best self, it becomes paramount that we use our minds differently and think differently. Our minds want to see proof before they admit that anything has arrived. If we can take the vibrational frequency of where we are, regardless, and spin it up to highest alignment, we will be in the Vortex. Feelings of appreciation for everything, wanted or unwanted, and love of all bits of creation regardless of what is occurring will get you into the Vortex.

There are verses in the Bible that could be cited to validate some of what I have said, but the feelings that are vibrating you into the Vortex defy any religion. You do not have to have any religious beliefs to feel the feelings that will get your vibrational frequency into the Vortex. Abraham Hicks tell us that when you appreciate where you are at any given time and hold those thoughts of appreciation for as little as seventeen seconds, other things to appreciate will appear and the feelings will become stronger and stronger. In as little as sixty-eight seconds of holding those thoughts, your point of attraction will shift enough that manifestation will start. When the mind can accept that manifestation is possible it becomes much easier to accomplish.

If there is something you desire, and your mind goes back and forth causing you to worry and replay all the aspects of why you can or can't get this, you are slipping out of the Vortex. At this point your thoughts are making you very counterproductive. Our Universe is one of inclusion. When we are offered something we can say, "No, thanks, I don't want that." Sentient beings are able to refuse something that is offered. The Universe, however, refuses nothing. If you want in your life money to go on a trip, as an example, but you think and focus on your lack of money for the trip, you are in "Universe Speak" saying, "Yes, bring me this lack." In order for you to manifest your desires, what is referred to these days as the Law of Attraction, you have to know without a doubt that it is coming and you have to live your life as though your desire is already there. In this example, you would need to start making plans, etc.

Most people do not believe to this degree. Most would say, "Okay, I will try that." They would however in their minds be saying, "Yeah, like this is going to work," and they would be doubting. Within that doubt is the vibration that will deny the desire. The person will then discount the entire law, just because it didn't work for them when in all actuality it was their own thoughts that kept the money for the vacation away from them.

This is the mind part of the mind/body/spirit triad. As we learn to work with our mind and learn how to think in a way that will encourage our best self to emerge, we will become more of a master of our fates rather than a victim of our whims. One way that our minds can help us is to work on our daily affirmations. One of the most powerful and helpful things that I learned on my journey to my best self came from Dr. Wayne Dyer. He shared with his readers that the most important parts of the day are those five minutes before we go to bed and the five minutes after we wake up. As you reflect on the day, be appreciative for as many things as you can think of. Repeat your affirmations, whatever they are, three or four times. This repetition sets you up successfully because manifestation and drawing things to your life stop when we are asleep. When you wake up, repeating the affirmations and looking forward to the day regardless of where it goes will set you up for a glorious experience. When you take this advice and couple it with the teachings of Eckhart Tolle, who tells us to live in the "now," you are preparing your surroundings and your life in a way that will encourage a high vibrational frequency.

As I was influenced by my reading in my effort to assimilate the changes of view and changes in thinking, this is one thing that helped me the most. I became aware of the teachings of Abraham as channeled by Esther Hicks. They had suggestions about the necessity for a way of thinking to raise vibrations in order to attract to you things that you desired. The combination of the two avenues gave me an enhanced life experience. I allowed a sad experience of the death of a friend to throw me in a tailspin. The ironic thing is that this friend provided the defining experience that led to a more enlightened life. It was during this time of grief of loss that my balance was thrown off kilter. It is that imbalance I have been working on gaining once again. I find that focusing on change by working on my vibrations is only a part of it, and I need to be more fully engaged in my daily affirmations.

An affirmation goes beyond positive thinking. Your affirmation is a statement of who you are. Examples of mine are as follows:

I am generous. I am kind. I am compassionate.

I am appreciative of all of life's experiences.

I am living a life of love and abundance.

I am a creative, successful author.

I am in a loving relationship.

I am experiencing a cosmic, eternal, connection to spiritual energy that is unconditional love and has been reunited through lifetimes.

I am love, I am sunshine, and I am a gift to all who meet me.

I am beautiful, and I am experiencing this life in the perfect body.

Your affirmations will be your own. Every time you begin a sentence with the words, "I am," you are unleashing your Source power. You are aligning yourself with the power of creation. You are establishing who you really are. If you say that you are mad, it will follow that you are mad. If you choose, you can be happy and fulfilled. It is something to be aware of and practice. Once you have your affirmations, you will need to live them. Know that what you say you are is what you are, already, now, in this instance. It is and will always be this way.

We have said over and over that we cannot control our thoughts. We can, however control which thoughts we will focus on. Focusing on positive thought is not all that is necessary. We must also be willing to act in a way that is not counter- productive. In other words, if our thoughts and our actions are not the same, we will not be in balance. Let us say that we believe that everyone should be treated equally but exclude some groups from our acceptance. We will not be living authentically and we will not reflect our best self. The example I will use here is a current dilemma: the current battle for marriage equality. People can voice that they are in favor of the LGBT community being treated fairly until they want to have the right to marry. Then it becomes a dance around terminology and you quickly see that equal doesn't mean equal in their eyes. They are not being authentic. They are professing one belief and living another.

No matter what quality, issue, or belief you have, if you do not live in accordance with your actual beliefs you are not being authentic. You are reflecting the ego's view and not the spirit view. When we are living our lives as our best self, we are being authentic in every situation. It is often said we are being true to ourselves. It is at this point that we issue a disclaimer, however. I have had instances recently when I was angry about a situation. There was someone in my family that I was relating this irritation to, simply (to my way of thinking) venting, getting it out of my system, and letting it go. She questioned why I was angry when I was supposed to be happy all the time and not get angry. Obviously she doesn't understand what striving to be our best self is about. When we live authentically and are angry, we can express our anger. To balance our life, however, we cannot hold on to the anger. It can be expressed, accepted, and let go. This is how it is handled in the way it needs to be handled to stay in balance and to live an authentic life that reflects our best self.

There are so very many ways that we reach a state of imbalance and many of them, actually most of them, revolve around the mind and how we have conditioned it to think and react. If we continue to think the way we that we thought when the problem was created, it will continue to be a problem. If we are ever going to change a current situation, we will have to deal with it in a different way and that quite often begins with our thoughts about the problem.

You have your own set of problems and irritations. We will always have issues. We will have problems that are easily solved and dealt with. We also have situations that appear to be resolved but pop up again. I find that for me, personally, most of the latter type of situations have to do with family issues. Sometimes if we are going to stay in balance we need the help of others to show us solutions that we might not otherwise see on our own. For example, when my daughter was partaking in certain activities that I disapproved of, I struggled with my inability to stop her participation. It was then that I went to Al-anon. That organization is for the friends and families of alcoholics and others with addictive behaviors. This organization, however, is extremely beneficial for helping anyone detach from behavior and to understand how you are, in your effort to care, actually enabling poor behavior to continue. It is a way to deal with issues. You may find that private counseling is an area you want to pursue and there are many good life coaches that offer their services. Whatever the direction you take, if it helps you, personally, balance your life, it is a step well-taken.

One thing has become clear during this last month. Once I established a firm resolve to get balanced again, I made only decisions that served me. I gave up depending upon others to help me at their leisure but rather I took others out of the equation. If I needed help with a particular task, I found someone specifically for that task. It was during this resolved time that I found a passion that I had thought was elusive, in the form of a creative expression. We usually think of passion as it relates to a vibrant physical relationship. Vibrational passion when you are cosmically and eternally linked to the energy of another person is indescribable. Because of the intensity of such a meeting of vibrations and energy, it is extremely spiritual but it is raw, and it makes you feel like you are sending sparks out because you cannot contain them all within your space. You relate to that person whether you are in their personal space or not. It is an intensity, a longing, and ache that you think can never be soothed. You begin to feel the essence of the other essence in all ways at all times. The sight of that person will spin your vibrations. While you may desire a physical expression of that ultimate, cosmic, eternal, vibrational alignment, it is only because as physical beings that is the closest we can be connected. Dialogue and commitment to merge the creative energy will result in conflict within, if you allow it to. When you accept the "nowness" of the situation and realize that the energy, vibration, and feelings far override a brief physical mergence, you can transcend into a higher level of consciousness that is pure love. It is however the physical tension that can fuel the vibrational energy, thus expanding the feelings even more. If you do not have a way to creatively express the dynamics that have been created, I imagine a person would implode in some way.

We need a great deal of discussion to get a working relationship when we find ourselves in a position where one party could have both the physical and vibrational relationship and the other person is not free to make that commitment. It is a mental exercise that will, in the end, have to balance with the body (sexual) and the spirit (vibrational energy). My writing partner and I both realize that to pursue a physical relationship within the realms of our realities would not add to the creative essence we share, but would rather detract from it. We both crave the creative, all-encompassing feelings of passion that is present when we collaborate and co-create. We know that if we can keep this energy funneled, there is nothing we cannot create, and we will do it more successfully than we either could ever have imagined because there is no other way it can be. It is a synergistic occurrence. We realize that physical relationships change, constantly, but pure vibrational alignment that reflects cosmic, eternal love will never dissipate, it will only intensify. But be assured, if it ever happens to you, there will be a degree of actual physical ache and unrest that will have to be dealt with if you are to stay in such close creative contact.

In this particular time in my life, I am self- aware enough to deal with issues that even as recently as five years ago, I did not even know existed. Once you truly embrace the reality that you are a vibrational, spiritual being in a physical body you view the world differently.

My writing partner, with whom I am creating a fictional novel, is my manifestation of passion. I thought when I was manifesting passion it would be a physical love affair. It is so much more intense than I would have thought, but it is the ultimate manifestation because he is the vibrational alignment that is a mirror of mine. We have amassed energy from other lifetimes, and we have found each other in this lifetime. We "recognize" each other and while time will tell, I am sure that we will be content in our association because we (the defining energy that is "us") will not want to leave each other in this lifetime. It is beyond physical expression. I will say this because I think it will help you. This is not a statement to be submitted to judgment, but if you judge, that is on you. With Art and me, there is an "us" that is just as real as any physical relationship or marriage. It is a 'marriage" of energy. It is a separate entity that has nothing to do with any relationships that either of us has on the physicality of this incarnation. It is an entity that is indefinable by a physically based existence that we are all aware of. It is when you transcend the physical that you enter into this vibrant existence. I have never experienced it earlier in life and I am thankful because I would never have been able to absorb it. I have experienced relationships where I was aware that we had met and interacted before, but never this intensely. The balance occurs when you recognize the beauty and completeness of this kind of energetic union. It is a choice every time we meet someone, anyone, how we will choose to interact with them. When we meet someone in that indefinable way that leads us to know we have known them before, we can then choose creative, vibrational, energetic, cosmic, eternal love over a brief physical union. In the end, we are balancing the yin and the yang. It occurs with some people, but is seldom discussed.

We are going to have to wrap our minds around the fact that we create our lives. We are usually under the impression that life just happens. That we are the recipient of either good things or bad things. That is not the case at all. We draw everything to our experience. Our life is the result of our vibrational alignment with what comes into it. If our life is to change, we have to learn to adjust our vibrations by shifting our true feelings in a way that will increase our vibrational offerings to the universe.

The body is a magnificent pod that is a way to harness a bit of the source energy that we are allowed to experience in this incarnation. We are more than just this little bit. We are always seeking to be free of the "pod" constraints. Our consciousness sleeps until a series of circumstances cause us to awaken and look around knowing what we are here for. We are here to experience joy. We are here to have fun and experience all that life has to offer. We have desires that provide the edge of a cliff. If we are brave enough to jump, we can experience a life that will allow our soul to fly. It is all vibrational.

We knew this when we arrived here. Our spirit overrides everything until the age of about five when we begin noticing our conditioning and environment. The more our pod ages, the further we get away from the true self that is vibrational source energy that is love. We continue this way until there is a defining moment presented that allows us to begin remembering who we are. This moment is not by chance. It is a moment that could not be chance because it awakens us. Once that happens, our life changes and we could not go back to a sleepy existence, even if we wanted to.

As you can see, the mind and how we use it can make a world of difference in our lives and what we experience. When our mind creates and accepts everything as a gift, with appreciation to the universe for providing the experience, our vibrations will be at their highest and we will draw unto us all that we desire. So much of what I am relating to you in this book has been written by others many times, and I will find myself repeating certain parts also. When we work to create a balance in our own essence, for lack of a better word, there is a constant need for us to remind ourselves of the very things that we need to recall in order to be free.

When you get in a place of total vibrational alignment, your world becomes so different. If one were to observe my life as they perceive it, it would appear very simple. It is, on an observable level. On a vibrational level, I have never been more creatively inspired. I have never had a reason to direct unconditional love into a creative direction. I have never before felt such unconditional love from energy emanating from another recognizable energy source. I am still working my mind around the experience. But, and this is a big one, if I allow my mind to try and use the logic of the physical world, I will reach the wrong conclusions. I have to allow myself to just feel. Accept and feel right now. When we do that, it is what it is and all is well. There is no other way. It is a relationship that cannot be quantified and explained physically. It is accepted totally, unconditionally, and is recognized as a reunion of spiritual, eternal, everlasting love.

I have attempted to divide this book on balance into separate areas but realize that this is never able to be done. We can talk about them separately but we cannot experience them separately. We are talking about experiencing anything in a balanced approach with all three aspects contributing to the experience. If we let our mind override our body and spirit, we will create imbalance, and so it is with any other combination of the three.

If, in any situation, you use your mind to think about all of the different possible scenarios, the reasons something is happening, and put your imagination to use in a certain way, you can literally create your own Hell. I know this because I have done this before in my life. I have taken one small instance, let's say, someone running late. I have imagined them in a car wreck, imagined them blowing our meeting off, letting them ignore our date and blow a relationship off. One rarely uses their thoughts and minds for a better feeling. If you are going to be a balanced, happy, fulfilled individual, you must stop this destructive penchant for using the imagination to create what you do not want. Our imagination is one of the most impressive of all of the gifts our source gave to us to help us create our reality, and when we learn to use it, our spirit will literally fly through life, and our physical pod will be the recipient of untold dreams that come true.

We are going to imagine our life into the fulfillment of a desire. We should imagine the life we want, and you will each do this in your own way. If, for instance, you imagine a life of wealth, it is a subjective value. Wealth for some is a nice home, a nice car, food on the table and money to pay bills with ease. For some it is a million dollars in the bank. And, for some, it is vast amounts of money and possessions. But, for this exercise, I am going to use my recent invitation into the world of writing a novel. I establish my affirmations. It will take a while to get the precise wording because you will get what you ask for whether you realize it or not. Precision will help direct the intent and pinpoint the desire more accurately:

182

I am enjoying the success of having a best- selling novel with over a million copies sold.

I am enjoying traveling with my writing partner, Art, as we conduct radio and personal interviews.

I am anticipating the television talk show path with my writing partner as we discuss the books and the upcoming movie that is in the works.

I am working with Art to expand our novels into a more popular series.

I am enjoying the freedom that the sale of these books is providing.

You can see how this works. This is my list of affirmations. In this same frame of reference, Art's list of desires might be entirely different. We can both draw into our own existence what we want. If it is the same thing, we will both experience it. If there are different things, we will both experience a part of the whole in a different way.

Now, we put the imagination to work, which is the really fun part. We live our lives as though we already have achieved our desires. One of the first things I did, within a week of beginning our collaboration, was to design a simple book cover. It has since been created. It was created in a roundabout "meeting" on Facebook. Art had the concept, we shared it with the artist, and it was created. It came to life in our minds, and because we had known it was accomplished, it came to be. This visualization was actually a tip that was in one of Wayne Dyer's books that worked well for me in my own writing. Once you see the cover of a book, it becomes a reality. You are just working toward that reality. You don't question it because it already exists. This is how you use the imagination to create what you do want. I see us walking up on stage, excitedly, with smiles on our faces. Our combined energies are dancing around and creating a far-reaching excitement in the audience. This vision is a done deal once we imagine and absorb the reality. It is an exercise. It is a way to attract into your life that is which you want. You do this day after day, week after week, with no doubt that you are getting closer and closer to those successes. You do not worry about the why, where, or when of your desires, you just put yourself in a place, vibrationally, that allows you to receive what you have asked for. When you achieve this alignment, there is no other way for life to happen. Art and I discussed this aspect of our work and quickly agreed that we were intended to meet up in this way in order to create. The book is our creative offering to the universe, the celebration of our energy reunited and strengthened in this incarnation. It is a united vibrational offering and because of that, our vibrations are aligned with our desires of a successful, money-making best-seller. He has an outline in his mind of a trilogy and we have discussed the direction of books two and three. Because of the topic and its pertinence in today's events in the country and the world, we can even see it as a movie.

I am using my experience as an example so that you can see how this process works. When we allow others, our friends and our best meaning family members, to tell us all the reasons that it will not turn out the way we envision it, we begin to worry and stew and start sending out conflicting messages in the Universe... "I want this, I don't think this will happen, but I want it to," this is why most of our dreams elude us. When you can send out the dream, use your imagination to let your feelings know you already have it, and relax, knowing it is on its way, you can't miss. It will happen.

While I have covered quite a bit of different areas, the overriding factor is how everything will help us keep a balanced life that will reflect our best selves. I read over my recent work and started laughing. I am living the life I have always dreamed of. The depth of my experiences are giving me a vibrational high, and I just realized that I wasn't even aware of it. I had been looking at specific items coming to me in a particular way, and totally missed the arrival of something even better and more fulfilling. My mind was so focused in one direction that it did not see the meteoric arrival of all that I have dreamed of. Having realized this, I am elevated to a higher vibration still.

If you are still pondering the idea of a best self, it is not difficult to achieve. My best self is one that has given up judgment, criticism and condemnation. That does not mean that I never judge, criticize or condemn. What it means is that I am extremely aware of when those old habits occur. I quickly find a way to counteract those thoughts with better thoughts, and every day I am better in avoiding those behaviors. I am kinder, more compassionate, more empathetic, more generous, more appreciative and thankful. It is a smoother way of living. There is less strife and stress. I no longer allow my ego to dictate what I think of as right or wrong. I choose happiness over being right. I don't make a judgement on things that are good or bad. And last, but certainly not least, I allow everyone to follow their own path. In addition, I have learned to use the Law of Attraction in a way that will allow me to draw into my life the things that I wish to have. This use is something that is easier to talk about than to successfully practice because there are so many outside influences that can distract you in the Law of Attraction. My best self allows that every day is wonderful regardless of what happens. I know that whatever happens is something that needs to happen in order for something else better to happen.

DAYS SIXTY THROUGH NINETY

Before we decide what and how the next four weeks will be spent, we will reflect on what has happened in these last two months.

One of my decisions was to use my diet in a way that reflects better choices of food. I was going to add foods that were raw and unprocessed and take as many processed foods away as possible. I have eaten no gluten, and little dairy and sugar. I have also added more water and limited my caffeine. I cannot tell that my weight or size has changed but I feel much better, less stressed, and happier. When we are concerned about true balance we know that happiness and joy are the goals.

Another thing that I was going to focus on was the inside and outside of my house. I have engaged someone to help me clean and organize on a weekly basis. I worked with a design studio to assess my current furniture and come up with a placement in all of the rooms. Taking note of what pieces needed to be removed, I began sorting through the pieces that served as storage. I got rid of some of it and donated it. I packed up and stored some other things. I will be moving items around and getting rid of three or four major pieces of furniture. I will be adding a couple of new pieces. The cleaning lady will then come weekly to help keep my new surroundings cleaning when my attention lags.

I called a landscape company to give an estimate of the front garden and they will be completing the work shortly. I will still have areas in the back yard that need attention, and I may save those until next spring, but I have a plan.

CONNECTING TO THE MENTAL ACTIVITIES

For my mind activities, I am working on sorting thoughts so that my vibrational health is at its optimum, and I am writing this book and co-authoring a suspense novel. If you read my previous book, "Confronting your Best Self" you can decide for yourself how differently the tone of the writing is. I am just getting the edited manuscript back to do the third draft, and I can see that there was a lack of upbeat information. The basis of the book was in sorting out conflict, in confronting issues, so it stands to reason that it would not be quite as light, but the issues that needed to be confronted are the very issues that now hold a balance in my life.

In the next month, the focus will be on the spiritual aspect of our mind/body/spirit persona. It is the part I love the most. I will use this time to share information that I originally discovered on my journey to my best self. It will not be a reiteration of my first book, but it will contain new information that will help you spiritually understand the importance and the power that you truly do possess and how this power can help live an inspired life on a higher plane. I will include some of the most pertinent and helpful parts if needed. I will work not from the idea of creating a best self but from the aspect of keeping that best self in balance. Any time you do work on the spirit, you cannot go wrong. It is when you ignore and abandon the inspired work that an imbalance is created.

For some people the word "spirit" calls them to think "spiritual" in the way of religion and they begin to associate this work with religious effort. The mind/body/spirit is not about religion, it is about something more. It is about the source of all that is, which is God. It is about being so connected to the source of "all that is" to actually be that source. As a part of the source, we are one with that source, which in essence means that the power of the whole is found within that part. We then become co-creators with that source. When we are spiritually and vibrationally aligned with this power, we will attract to us that which we desire and that which is on the same vibrational frequency.

We will know if we are vibrationally aligned with our spirit by how we feel. When we are living from a place of alignment, we will feel good. When we are not aligned, we will feel bad. When we have feelings of jealousy, anger, hatred, disgust, etc. we are working at lower vibrations and we will not feel good. When, however, we feel thankful, appreciative, generous, kind, and compassionate, we will feel great. We will be humming along in life. This does not mean that we will never have problems. It only means that we will not allow those problems to rob us of our happiness and joy in life.

Okay, time to get started with our soul work on this leg of our triad. Take a look at how you feel at the beginning of the day. When your wake up, are you generally in a good mood, looking forward to the day, or do you wake up dreading your days? Do you listen to more than thirty minutes of news? If so, how much? Which season is your favorite? Do you experience any different moods and feelings if the day is gloomy than if it is sunny? How do you feel when someone gets something that you have wanted for a long time? Do you feel like you have enough money or income? Are you satisfied with how you look? Do you like your home? How often do you take time off from work for relaxation?

Looking at the above questions can help you establish a bottom line for how your feelings are affecting your spirit connection. If you don't like to wake up, watch a great deal of news, do not like gloomy days, tend to be jealous when others get something new, never feel you have enough money, don't like how you look, wish you had a better house, and never take time to relax, you are definitely not feeling in spirit. Look at the opposite of these: You look forward to the day, don't listen to much news, take the weather as it comes, be happy for those who are able to get things they want, have enough, are at least okay with your looks and your home, and take time to relax, you are operating in a greater state of inspiration.

That being said, if you can learn to think of a gloomy day as being bad, you can relearn those feelings. You can change your thoughts about that gloomy day and in the changing of the thoughts, the gloomy day will begin to appear differently to you. No matter what you are looking at, it can be perceived differently. We know this because there are many people who are not affected by the weather conditions. The only reason for this difference is that they are focusing their attention to enjoying their day regardless of the weather. (There is a diagnosable disorder called SADD, or seasonal affective disorder, which can reflect those negative emotions. I am not addressing that illness nor directing this refocusing effort toward the people who suffer from it. It is real but it can be eased by medication and the use of specific kinds of lighting.)   Since we have no control over the weather, it is totally futile to even consider that it can ever be anything other than just what it is. That being the case, why would we allow something that we can do nothing about to so seriously affect us? The answer is that we do not have to. We simply have to change the way that we think about a gloomy day.

When you have a gloomy day, take time to think of all of the activities you can do. Do not think of what you cannot do, just the ones you can do. When you finish, you will see the list is a pretty long one. If you think about it, there are things that you can do on a gloomy day that you would not do on a sunny day. While it is true that usually the more enjoyable activities can be done on a sunny day, the more recreational things gloomy days are allocated a very important task. They are the days that will help you catch up with indoor hobbies. Years ago, Dr. Norman Vincent Peale told us to change our thoughts and we would change our world.

Dr. Wayne Dyer has a book written on the subject of changing your thoughts and changing your life.

You are the one in charge of your life. This is one of the easiest things to tell a person, but when you begin to do that, there are always others around who don't want to see that change you might make. These are people who are not comfortable in their own skin nor are they comfortable with their life experiences. They feel that because their life is not going as they wish, then neither should yours, so they keep telling you why you can't do this and can't do that. They will thwart you at every corner in order to keep you from achieving happiness. It isn't because they don't care about you. It is because they want to be in charge of their life, too, and they don't know how.

I am not certain who gets the credit for this quote, but I feel it is a wonderful jumping place for a discussion that will lead to encouraging balance. "A flower does not think of competing with the flower next to it. It just blooms." The plant world may compete as far as seeking nutrients, water, and space, the things needed to survive, but you never have a daffodil wondering if they are as good as a rose. The rose doesn't put down the poison ivy as being less significant. Now, humans may judge the plants and categorize them but we need to remember when dividing weeds and acceptable plants what Ralph Waldo Emerson told us, "A weed is simply a plant whose values have not been recognized," or words to that effect. The problem with that definition is that it would undoubtedly take the wonderful dandelion out of the weed category and place it into the valuable plant category. We are as guilty of judging plants and animals as we are in judging ourselves. When we can allow ourselves to be what we are and who we are and know that is enough we can open up within us total balance with very little effort.

We have covered much but there is still much to cover. I have turned back to enjoy some of the YouTube offerings of one of my favorite spiritual venues, Abraham Hicks. The premise of the Hicks' teachings revolve around the idea that we are all vibrational creatures and we vibrationally align with all that comes into our lives, good or bad. When we align with whatever it is that we want, it will be attracted vibrationally to us. We ask for what we want, align the vibrations and create a point of attraction, and allow it into our existence. There are all sorts of nuances to gain the power of this Law of Attraction. It is a universal law and it is at work all the time. When we become aware of it and decide to try to use it in the way that provides us with our desires, we really need to do our homework if we are to be successful. We need to learn up exactly how to ask. We need to create affirmations and operate our vibrations so that we are releasing resistance. It sounds complicated, but it is simply letting our desires fly out to the Universe and know that the Universe is taking care of it.

When we are keeping our spiritual alignment in balance with the mind and body, there are different areas of thought that we need to explore. We operate under the idea that the body is as we think we see it. It really isn't. I have often said that I have no clue about how I really appear to someone else. I have an extremely skewed view of myself. I have been told that I have pretty eyes therefore when I look in a mirror I perceive my eyes as being a pretty feature of mine.

Now, we come to what the meaning of the word pretty is. When we begin talking about looks, it all becomes so subjective. For our purposes, however, I will accept that I have pretty eyes. I have also been told that my hair is pretty therefore I accept that feature as being one of my better features. I also know that I have a good brain and I am smart. I do not claim to be the brightest bulb in in the box but I possess an above average intellect. This is also subjective because, as a teacher, I saw very average ability students far out do supposedly bright students.

That too can be based on your view. So, we have areas where we are judged and based on those judgments, we begin to accept the word outside of us as being a fact.

This might not be too bad if all of the messages we received were those that would make us feel good, but they are not. Many of the messages children receive are about their poor behavior or areas where they fall short of someone else's expectations. Then, to make matters worse, we grow up and keep playing the tapes over and over, and the believing of these subjective judgments cause us not to feel good, but rather to usually feel badly about ourselves.

If there is a problem with the Law of Attraction, it is that it is presented as some kind of magic pill that we can just throw out there and, Poof! Our wish is granted, kind of like a Genie in a bottle. When it doesn't work that way, people get upset and say that it doesn't work. It is always working. It is always giving you something that matches your vibrational offering. To attract what you are wanting you must do it consciously rather than by default. It has worked for me several times so I know that is does work. I have shared some of those times in previous books so I will not use old examples. I will use an example that is fresh and probably the most powerful thing that has ever happened to me.

Two years ago, as I was finishing my first book, I was working with the Law of Attraction in my life and decided I would attract a man into my life, a helpmate, a friend. I knew that the years I had spent out of a relationship of any kind made this desire to have a man back in my life a bit disconcerting. I have been divorced over thirty years and while there was one long term relationship in that time, I have lived with no one besides my ex-husband. The idea of having someone around all the time did not really appeal to me. My affirmations, then, were as follows:

1. I am in a loving relationship with a caring man who makes me laugh and laughs along with me.

2. I am in a loving relationship with an interesting, intelligent man who encourages me and is not critical.

3. I am in a relationship that is built on mutual respect and shared goals

4. I am in a loving relationship with a man who enjoys spending time with me, excites me, and is excited to be a part of my life.

5. I am in a loving relationship with a man that goes wherever it goes and one I trust to reintroduce me to sex if that is what we decide to do.

6. I am in a loving relationship with a man who just wants a loving relationship, deep friendship, and does not want marriage but will be around occasionally, a friend to hang out with and enjoy life with.

7. I am in a loving relationship with a man who likes me exactly as I am.

Art is the manifestation of most of these desires. Before we got to working one day, I showed him this list, and he agreed with me that as the list was written, he was that manifestation. I always like to clarify, and he is a very generous male in that he doesn't roll his eyes at me, he listens and lets me bounce ideas and questions off of him and tries to answer as honestly as he can. We had waved and spoken for a while so I asked him two questions. The first was, "When did you first notice me?" He said that it was almost two years ago and gave me the month, it was October, 2013. He was aware of me to the point that he remembered the month and the day he first "recognized" me. And that, folks, is how it needs to be perceived when these kinds of things happen. It is a recognition of energy that you have previously been a part of, an eternal connected energy. The second question I asked was, "Why did you not come over before then? Why now?" He thought for a moment and said that it was just what he needed to do that day. That is because that is the day that he and I were resonating our vibrations equally. We were, at that time, reconnecting with our non-physical beings and recognizing the non-physical being of the other. His energy was more in tune than mine. He was recognizing and sending vibrations which I received sometimes and sometimes not. Once he and I were both emitting on the same vibrational frequency, our meeting was no surprise. When we come from the non-physical into the physical world, we still are non-physical beings. We will interact with many other energies and all of the energies will be amassed within a person. It is when the energy and the vibrations match that you have strong, immediate, and undeniable attraction. Because we are in physical pods, we react physically, but that reaction does not always stay. It is when the energies and vibrations are such that they continue to vibrate that we establish the relationships that endure.

I would like to take this time to clarify that we have been working together creating a fictional novel, the first in a series. We have become business partners and it is a working relationship that holds many of our dreams in the balance. We have completed a full novel in about ten weeks and are currently editing and rewriting. We have established some filming of promotionals and have legally established a partnership arrangement. Our energy is focused on the creative aspect of our lives, and it is causing vibrations that are allowing request after request to come to us quickly and easily. It has been a phenomenal experience for both of us.

Now, it also serves as a wonderful example for balance. We humans are strange creatures indeed, once we enter "the pod." A spiritual friend asked me to clarify this term when I was talking to her, and I told her that was how I referred to this physical body we are inhabiting. She liked it and responded with, People of Dreams, Depth, and Dimension. I loved that description, because it fits the term "pod" to a tee. We are spiritual, non-physical, eternal vibrational energy housed in a physical body or "pod." To keep our mind/body/spirit balanced, we must make them work together in such a way that there are no overriding problems with any one area. The best way to do this is through the acceptance of everything that comes your way. If you cannot accept what is happening in your life, you will become so off balance that what used to work will no longer work for you. As in the example above, if I allow the unrest about even one portion of this relationship to outweigh any other aspect, then I am creating an imbalance. Another thing to remember about balancing is that we are the ones responsible. I can expect no one to solve my balance but me.

The other day I was thinking about vibrations and thought that it would be so much easier if I were at a place where others actions didn't cause me to feel a bit down. I then was reminded that the mythical "they" weren't responsible for that, I am. I was allowing my negative thoughts to creep in. Once you become conscious, you will recognize negativity more easily and you will correct it more quickly. When we work with raising our vibrations and keeping them at a higher level, we unlock our potential for manifestation. This is what Art and I did with the affirmations we created earlier that had to do with the success for our book. We are often so focused on looking for a good life that we miss all the good moments. When we try to fit our experiences in a box and label it, we miss being free to live a wonderfully exciting life. We will constantly miss opportunities to vibrate at those higher frequencies that will get us into the Vortex and keep us there.

If I am constantly focusing on what I think might be missing from any experience, I am denying what I attracted. I am denying someone the pleasure of the gift they are giving me with their presence. We are put into other's lives for a reason. We attract those who enter so, in essence, we have invited them into our experience. We then will say, "Oh, wait, you are not what I want." As Art and I both have discussed, I had set in a motion of affirmations and vibrations which were matching with his vibrations and that was when he noticed me in Panera. We noticed each other and spoke and acknowledged each other for almost two years before he came to speak to me, and when that happened, the energy and vibrations were so in alignment and so strong that we "recognized" each other and began a unique and unusual friendship/relationship/partnership that does not fit into a box. We can both look at that relationship and see that if we expect it to fit into some category or another, we will both be disappointed, because it doesn't. He said early when we were talking a phrase I use often myself, "it is what it is." Truer words were never spoken. When we add the wisdom of Eckhart Tolle to the teachings of Abraham Hicks, we come up with a vibrational relationship that works extremely well for both of us when we stay in the present moment. No one knows what the future will bring because we are constantly vibrating and sending out our desires. With all of our technology, we cannot predict the weather so we certainly cannot what will happen between any two people at any time.

If we focus on the part of any relationship we have, the very fact that we give attention to, causes some kind of a vibration to begin. We must remember that if you are working on vibrations to help you stay balanced, you will need to focus on what makes you feel good. As long as you are focusing on the thoughts, activities, and attitudes that make you feel good, you are feeling your way to a vibrational vortex in which the things you want come to you.

Let us create an example of sorts. Our child is sick and needs the comfort of a parent or grandparent. We can become, for that brief moment in time, the most important person in that child's life. When we choose to do this, we are giving a gift to that child that cannot be taken away. I have done this myself. I have kept both of my grandchildren when they have been sick, and I think I have been nurturing. Recently I inadvertently did just the opposite and it gave me a bad feeling after I realized what had happened, letting me know that I had learned a lesson I hope will make my next experience very different. Elijah had called me early one morning wanting to spend the night. I had just awakened and told him that I didn't know yet, if he wanted to ask me and if he wanted an answer now, it would be "no." Evidently, for whatever reason, I either said this sharply, or he was in a state where his feelings were to be hurt easily because that is what happened. He quickly went to tears and, of course, I was given the role of being at fault. I was sorry I had caused him sadness, but all of the explanations would not change it. I simply needed to file that for future reference. We cannot always "fix" things. We can only learn from our mistakes. Keep in mind when we have a chance to interact with anyone, we are a gift. We need to decide what kind of a gift we are going to be.

The second issue is that we have errands that we needed to do. Were these new errands or were they errands that had been put off. One of the biggest problems that confront us when we are thrown off balance is procrastination. While Benjamin Franklin is often given credit for this quote, it actually belongs to Philip Stanhope, Fourth Earl of Chesterfield, "Never put off till tomorrow what you can do today." When we put off anything, we run the risk of letting chores mount up until they are unsurmountable. My earlier attempts in balancing are a perfect example. I had put off chores and put off chores until I had to call help in to get the jobs done. We listen, for a time, then we seem to forget. It is when we become committed to the issues of balance that we will quit procrastinating and do jobs a little bit at a time.

The third issue is also, most probably, a result of procrastination. When we put off chores like going to the grocery store, you may find that you will be eating some rather strange combinations of food. I think this does not happen as often to households where there are children than it does with single adult households. I can avoid going to the grocery store for a week at least, but if anyone drops in, the cupboards are bare and I am embarrassed. I try to keep enough food handy that I am at least covered for two weeks whether I go to the store or not. I mention this because if we do not take care of simple chores like going to the grocery store, we can find out bodies out of sync with our mind and spirit and the ensuing imbalance can cause more problems than taking care of the shopping chore when it needs to be taken care of.

Now that we have looked at the issues, we can see that, when nothing can be done today to correct anything, we can just allow it. This is the way it is at this moment. No matter how aggravated or irritated we are, we can only allow it, there is no other option. The only need is to make sure these sets of circumstances do not occur on a regular basis. You also will realize that sometimes there are going to be glitches in life. We will never have perfect lives, and I am not sure what perfect even means. What would be perfect for you would not be perfect for me. Therefore, does perfect really even exist anywhere? Remarkable clarity happens when you realize that everything is perfect. What exists is a life that is perceived perfectly. When you perceive your life as being perfect, it is.

So, with the secret uncovered here, it becomes necessary to look at our lives seeing and feeling exactly like what we want it to be and it will be just that. Individual, isolated events may not be perfect, but don't be guilty of looking for such a good life that you ignore all the good moments. When we live in the "now," we will do what needs to be done and take care of what needs to be taken care of. When we procrastinate, what we are actually doing, in essence, is saying that there will be another, better time to do whatever it is that needs to be done. When we realize that there is no other time but now, we will no longer procrastinate. Think about this and apply it in a concrete example. Let us use the grocery store. Is there ever going to be any "better" time to get groceries? There may be a less crowded time, and we can certainly choose that, but there will never any one time that is better than any other time for grocery shopping. When we are procrastinating, we are choosing the future which is not guaranteed and in essence does not exist yet over now, which is here.

We begin hearing when we are young that things now are not as good as they will be in the future. We tell children how much fun they will have at school next year. We get to looking forward to High school when we are in Middle school. We look forward to college while we could be having the time of our life in high school. We spend half of our time in college looking forward and thinking about what kind of a job we will get, where we will live, and what kind of car we'll drive in a non-existent future. All the while we are missing moments of now. These are moments that will never be recovered. The Universe is expanding never to be at exactly the place it is now. We have lost time while looking for more time. When we learn to look at our lives and have fun regardless of the circumstances, we are balancing our lives. When our lives are balanced we are able to enjoy ourselves more. We cannot make it one way or the other. We cannot try to decide balance first or enjoyment first. Make the act of balancing as enjoyable as the balanced life itself.

Not too long ago, I was sitting here contemplating this ONE--ONE mind you-- thing in my life that is bothering me, wondering how to successfully deal with it so as not to cause me to implode and THIS POPPED UP, "Perhaps the greatest of all illusions is that life could somehow be better than it already is."The Universe answered my problem. My life is exactly how I called it to be and it is, today, right now, the best life I have ever had. Trust in life to answer your questions if you will open yourself up to receiving them. So, let's all have some fun with it.

LOOKING AT OUR LIVES IN A BALANCED WAY

Coming up now is one of the big reveals. Your life is always balanced. What you perceive as an unbalanced life is a life that is vibrating in one frequency for a while then at another frequency for a while. You are not vibrating at a steady frequency. This happens for a variety of reasons. We begin realizing and recognizing who we are. We become excited and happy with life, content with all that we are and all we are given. This positive state works for a while with most of us and we begin noticing certain things in our life are not what we thought they were because we have other people telling us that there is a reason not to be happy. This negativity causes a wavering, or wobbling, of our vibrations. We begin to look not with our own hearts, but with the eyes and ears of others. We then feel conflicted and have to work to confront the issues that are causing us to waver. The wavering and the imbalance of frequency is what causes us to feel imbalanced. The balance is always there, the ability to self-correct our frequency is always there. We only need to sit back and listen to the quiet and let our lives all fall back into place.

Balancing is simple once we access our ability to balance. Just as changing our thoughts is a learned experience, so is learning to balance. We are free to determine what we want to hang on to and what we want to release. Do we want to hang on to irritation or do we want to release it and allow ourselves to slow down and enjoy the experience of getting groceries? While it isn't one of my favorite chores, if I approach it by taking my time looking over produce, enjoying the sights of the foods at the deli, or whatever, then it will not seem like quite such a chore. Very often, I know, you are hurried and when that happens, you are vibrationally out of alignment and the chore becomes an irritation. If you change your idea about the chore, the vibration will change and your feelings about the chore will change. Then you will be in balance once more. To be in balance does not mean that you look forward to all of those pesky chores, it simply means that you acknowledge the chore as significant now.

Once we know how to get to our best self, it is easier to get back to our best self. We cannot beat ourselves up when we become imbalanced. If we do that, we become even more off center. Just realize imbalance is going to happen. Balance and imbalance are natural swings in life.

While we have not gone the original ninety days as of yet, it will be a good time to catch up on what is going on with my balancing activities. Now is a good time for you to review your notes and see where you are with your activities. Are there additional issues you have added? Make accurate assessments and don't sugar coat any lack of progress on your part. However things are falling into place is exactly where they are supposed to be. It is in the imperfection that we find perfection. It is in the incongruities that we find peace. It is in the achievement that we find our focus.

This post from Facebook I found to be very relaxing as I was easing the anxiety of balancing. Until I realized how easy it actually is to balance I was trying to hurry the process. I hope it helps you as much as it did me.

"I want to live simply. I want to sit by the window when it rains and read books I'll never be tested on. I want to paint because I want to, not because I've got something to prove. I want to listen to my body, fall asleep when the moon is high and wake up slowly, with no place to rush off to. I don't want it to be governed by money or clocks or any of the artificial restraints that humanity imposes on itself. I just want to be, boundless and infinite."

The author is unknown but somehow I think that person was very enlightened and aware of how wonderful a simple life can be.

Another point to be discussed when balancing is simplicity. The more we try to cram into our life, the more we find ourselves off balance, or rather maybe I should say, the easier it is to become off balance. We divide ourselves and our activities into days and nights and weekdays and weekends. We put each activity, chore, and job in certain boxes (yes, again with the boxes). When there are too many boxes for the space we have (our time frame) we stack boxes. When we stack them, the stack can become too high and some may fall over and spill out the contents then we have a mess to clean up. This is how we are living our lives these days. We think our children need to be in activities every night, and if one child is in two activities and another is in two activities and mom is in three activities and dad is in two activities and we have jobs and school in the mix, you can see very quickly that the boxes are stacking very quickly and we are over extending ourselves. Unless we are very aware of our feelings, we will begin to feel overwhelmed and that is low on the vibrational frequency scale. Overwhelmed feelings can rapidly deteriorate your vibrations. We can do one of two things to be in balance, and you will have to decide for yourselves which venue is right for you. You can organize your lives very closely and tightly and have a schedule that will cover all the areas. You can also simplify your schedule to allow free time for you and your family. Take the givens of job and school. Those cannot be changed. See if each family member can narrow down their activities to one, and you will go from nine activities to four activities. You will not give up everything but you will simplify and be able to enjoy the activities you are participating in at a more relaxed tone. The choice is yours and there are no wrong choices. Just be aware of choices and the feelings those choices bring about. Some people can deal with the stress of a tight schedule very well while others cannot.

Know yourself. Do whatever you need to do to keep yourself at the highest possible frequency.

We have talked about getting our life in balance and it dawned on me that while we are balancing our lives, we are also helping others balance theirs. When we are more balanced, we vibrate at a higher frequency. When that happens, others around us are affected, and their vibration can rise as a reaction to our increased vibration. Think about it a minute. When you are around someone who is happy and cheerful and seems to have a very positive outlook on life you usually feel better. Sometimes your vibrations are so far from theirs we find theirs annoying. That, too, is okay. It is an indicator that you are not vibrating on the same frequency and that their vibration is higher than yours. When we experience irritation over any subject, we know our vibrations are "off." Feelings are the indicators. Feelings are always the indicators of how well we are balanced. When we are balancing, we get ourselves in vibrations that encourage others to flit in and around to help us. One interesting example of this came just about thirty minutes ago as I was writing. I had a former classmate get in touch with me about a Facebook post that included me. His comments were very positive and gave me the oomph I needed at just that time to bump up my vibrations. He does not know this, but the Universe knew I needed it and he was the vessel in which it occurred. It will always happen that way for you. When you are sending out vibrations you will receive as needed what is needed.

As you have been reading about my work in this book, you have seen in a real way, I hope, that our lives are ever-changing. We begin doing one thing and we concentrate on that for a while then something else comes into our life and we shift our focus for a while. This is life. It is during the rush of life that we are called to find the best life we can have. We look forward to enjoying this life and doing it with the least amount of strife. It is not always easy because we listen to the droning of others as to how our life is to be. It is not supposed to work that way, but it often does and when we listen to others and try to live our life according to the whims of others, we are setting ourselves up for low frequency and imbalance. I am not telling you anything in this book you do not already know. I am not telling you anything you could not figure out on your own. What I hope that you take away from this book is that we are all free to choose as we choose without the judgment of others. We need to be in tune to our own desires and "follow our bliss" so to speak. We need to do those things in life that make our heart sing, and we will find that once we feel that feeling, we never want to settle for less than that feeling.

Now to take a look at where we are with our balancing as it concerns specific issues that we know and freely admit are out of sync. I had issues both inside and outside my home which are being addressed. There are bits of time taken daily to keep after the areas that are being addressed, with help, each week. It is often difficult for us not to want to rush to completion in any effort we are making to play "catch up" with something we have allowed to get ahead of us. If we slacked off of an issue for, let's say, six months, is highly unlikely that we can resolve the issue in six days or perhaps in six weeks. It may take us six months or longer because not only do we have the original problem, our lack of attention to it may have caused even more of an issue. The inside and outside are being well taken care of and making progress.

I have not made a clear cut between the mind and spirit. This is alright because much of what we work with when we are dealing with our spiritual self deals with the mind work that we do in regards to our spirit. Once again, when we accept that whatever happens is what is supposed to happen and what is happening is part of the plan the Universe has in mind to give us our desires, we can get into balance and maintain it.

One of the best lessons I learned when I was writing my first book and began working with the Law of Attraction was the importance and helpfulness of affirmations. When you are beginning any soul work it is important to decide what it is you want. I gave you a concrete example earlier but now is the time for us to come up with affirmations that will serve us well in the days to come. We need to begin to get our ideas flowing and cast our eyes on our desires. It does not matter what it is you are wanting. Some people are wanting money, and I confess that was my earliest desire that got me into the discovery of manifestation.

What I found was so very much more and that is what I am going to share in these next pages. It is a mind/spirit exercise. It will require you to learn to express your desires in a certain way that will add to your vibrational frequency and get you in a place that will allow that which you are seeking to come to you.

In order to start, I will reintroduce you to the words, "I am." Without going into the history of the power of these words, just think about how you already use those words. You will say, "I am tired," and you will feel tired. You may say, "I am excited," and your body will feel the excitement of the situation in question. Whatever follows those two words will unleash that very thing into the Universe as your desire and if you are in the vibrational alignment, it will come to you and be manifested. Once you release the desire, you must just let go. Allow the Universe to work into the how and why and when and where, all of the details are not yours to worry about. Your only job is to ask. If you want to get more detailed information about the use of the Law of Attraction than I give here (and I would strongly suggest that you read and view as much as possible about the teachings of Abraham Hicks. Go to YouTube and get to Abraham Hicks, and you will learn more and more about how vibrations help you.

Affirmations are verbal reinforcements, as I like to refer to them, to enhance your asking. They are directly related to the feeling of already possessing that which you wish, and they are stated as though you already are where you want to be and have what you want to have. I worked this week on some affirmations for my writing partner and me. We have yet to agree on the precise wording because if we are both working on the same project with the same goals in mind and vibrationally directed toward the achievement, it should come more easily or more quickly. Or, maybe not. However it comes will not matter. You can't second guess the Universe on how it delivers to us. You can only know that whatever we vibrationally align with will be what we get. Before I do this, keep in mind, JK Rowling, creator of the Harry Potter books, waited fifteen years before those books were published and twelve publishers turned her down... Your manifestations are not a hocus pocus magic genie-in-the-bottle manifestation. Patience with the faith that it will happen without a doubt is what will cause it to happen. With that in mind, I will give you the affirmations that we came up with that I believe will achieve our goals for success as it pertains to the current leg of my journey with my writing and my co-authoring with a partner.

1. I am enjoying the success of my "Your Best Life" series of books and the interviews and workshops it is garnering.
2. .I am in a great partnership where we are able to bounce ideas off of each other and add to the depth of the book as we write a bestselling, highly successful novel.
3. I am thankful for all of the ideas we get and all the doors that are opening for our creative endeavor.

4. I am thankful that the joined vibrational energy is creating a vortex where success is guaranteed.
5. I am seeing this success in many ways. I am seeing book signings, the travel, the interviews, and movie scripts that result from our success.
6. I am seeing the sales of this first book climb daily.
7. I am seeing a series of books with these characters.
8. I am absorbing the entire vibrational relationship I have with my partner to allow us to achieve all that we want.
9. I am only allowing into our experience observations, activities, and attitudes that will get us more deeply into that vortex of abundance
10. I am enjoying my success individually and in partnership.
11. I am thankful for everything I am experiencing.

These affirmations will be the way I will attempt to start every day and they will be the way I end every day. Whatever you decide you want to draw to you will be done in this way with your best feeling emotions guiding the allowing of it into your life. It will take practice, but it will be your final tool in leading a balanced life.

MAKING AFFIRMATIONS WORK FOR YOU TO ACHIEVE BALANCE

When we are discussing affirmations we need to be reminded that they are not exactly positive thoughts and repetitions. I have read much over the years about the power of positive thinking, and I believe that it is a very good bit of advice for us to think as positively as we can as often as we can. Affirmations are different in that we are affirming a statement to already be true. We are saying it in a way that enables us to believe it. Our subconscious does not know whether a statement is true or whether it is thought to be true. If we are told something about ourselves and we believe it, our subconscious will react as though it is true. It is when we give ourselves the statements of our life as we want it to be and act and believe on those statements that the Universe will respond accordingly and we will find experiences come to us that reinforce those beliefs.

When any of us look at our lives, we can focus on what is going on that is good. We can look at a specific interaction and see how enriching that interaction is in our lives, how productive it is, and how wonderful it helps us to feel. That is 95% amazing in how our soul (energy, vibrations, etc.) responds to it. Then, however, there is that 5% that we convince ourselves is lacking, and we let that perceived lack (which may or may not actually be true anyway) override the 95% amazing. We can look at every interaction with the 95% in our minds and hold that, or we can concentrate on the 5% and hold on to that. When we hold the 95%, we will thrive and we will be flowing downstream toward our dreams. When we hold the 5%, we are offering resistance so strong that our desires may never reach us. The choice is our every single day in every single situation.

Right now my life is in the downstream position with business and personal desires coming my way with a speed that is astounding me daily. This will continue as I focus on the 95% and not on the 5%. I was reminded in a meeting just yesterday that there were some instances where I was focusing on something I had never experienced and I kept reminding my subconscious that this was new and untried territory. The more I voiced it and the more I held to it, the more I was internally reminded of a perceived "lack," and that was delivering lack to me. When I realized that was what I was doing, I was able to adjust my messaging system and the very thing I had been dreading has become a source of anticipated activity. It really is that simple, but it takes practice and it takes a focus on making a true internal adjustment. We can't voice it, we have to feel it.

When we are balancing our lives to become our best self, we become a collector of tools that we need to help us along our journey. Three of our dearest tools on this journey are curiosity, imagination, and creativity. When we take our natural curiosity and let our imagination and creativity add the dimension needed, we create an almost supernatural ability to achieve our dreams. There has been story after story about instances where an imaginative and creative approach have made a difference in the reality of lives. When we focus on that imagined truth we draw the essence of it to us and a different reality is created for us because of it. I have had this happen in my life and as I continue to hold dreams in focus, I am continually achieving them. The more quickly I step out of my own way, the more quickly those dreams and desires come into my reality. We often find ourselves standing in our own way for the things we want most in life.

When you realize that everything works as it is supposed to work in the way it is supposed to work, you will realize that life is in balance already. When we consider our balance, we usually look from a societal viewpoint, not a spiritual one. We think about others looking at us in the same way we look at them. This is not the case. We reflect off of others how we perceive ourselves. If we think that someone judges us unfairly, it is because we are judging others unfairly. When we look at someone and make a snap judgement concerning anything about them, it is because that is what we are finding lacking in ourselves. We draw to us what we think. If we persist on dwelling on our perceived inadequacies, we will continue to draw those inadequacies. When we can change our perceptions, our entire reality will shift. When we feel beautiful, beautiful is how we are perceived. The reality of others is a reflection of our thoughts.

Balance occurs automatically when we get to the place where we realize that balance is not to be an effort, it is just to be realized. If we are having to "work" at anything within our inner self, we are sensing imbalance. When we release ourselves to the Universe, or Source, or God, we are giving up the need to control. When we give up the need to control outer circumstances, we settle into balance. It has taken me three years, three books, and about a quarter of a million words to get to this realization. It is as simple as being happy, just let yourself 'be"... Balance is just as simple, allow it. When you do, life will fall gloriously into place and you will know that "all is well."

When you realize that the only thing that matters in this world and in this life is that you are living a happy joyous life, you have achieved a balance that cannot be matched in any way by anyone.... ever. You will not be out of balance. If you sense that 'wobble" (as I like to call it) you can take deep breaths, listen to music, observe nature, meditate, do whatever it is you do to ground yourself and revel in the feeling of slipping back into the alignment that balance creates.

When you are in alignment and you are in a state of allowing all good things to come to you, you are in balance. The world around you can be in a state of chaos and events in your life can be downright nasty, but if you do not allow it to affect you vibrationally, you will stay in balance and you will be able to deal with those events on the outside much more easily.

Sometimes what we think and what we imagine causes us more turmoil than what is actually happening. We create much of our imbalance from a place of fear. We often fear the happiness we begin to feel when we are in alignment. We are afraid that it will not stay with us because it hasn't in the past. The reason it hasn't in the past is because we charged someone else with being keeper of our happiness. When we had expectations and they were met by someone else, we were happy. When they ceased to behave as we expected, we became unhappy. When we realize that it is not anyone else's job to make us happy, only ours and when we take that responsibility upon ourselves and deal with it on a vibrational level, we will experience happiness that remains. It is our happiness to keep.

When we take these steps, we realize our power. We now know that regardless of what the external situation becomes, we can do our inner work and we will come out ahead. There are times in life where the eternal situations are not easily discarded, but when that happens, we need to work daily to get to a better place in our thoughts and vibrations. It will happen, but we also need to allow ourselves to be as kind and compassionate to ourselves as we would be to others in the same situation and circumstance.

Final Thoughts on
the Secrets to Balancing Your Best Self

If you have followed the books in this series, you will already know what there is for you to do in order to balance yourself. Let me offer these affirmations for you to consider:

I will ---Look at your mood, your thoughts, your beliefs about yourself and decide if you are happy with them.

I will----Begin to become aware of your thoughts, deciding which ones are serving to help you "feel good" and which ones make you "feel bad."

I will ----Begin discarding those thoughts that make you feel bad.

I will ---Continue to consider your thoughts. Hold on to those that are uplifting and let go of those that are not serving to keep you in a positive and upbeat place.

Consider taking the following actions.

1. Begin to observe that as your thoughts are more carefully directed, you observe your life experiences changing.

2. Once you have realized that you are the one who directs your life, continue to do so.

3. If you find yourself faltering, as you will during times in your life as you begin your transformation, treat yourself gently and compassionately.

4. Reaffirm your commitment to yourself.

5. Begin the process over anytime you need to in order to keep attuned to what you have determined is your best self.

6. Look at all areas of your life and if there are some areas that feel good and some areas that feel bad, continue to delve deeply , change your thoughts about yourself and your situations, and watch your life improve.

The last step is simply to do both sets of steps over and over until they become how you think and react to situations and events in your life.

Our lives are always changing and so are we. When we realize this -- and know that events happen that are out of our control, we will come to be so evenly balanced that change will not cause us fear or worry. We know that the ultimate creator is still creating and that creation is coming through us. We come to know the eternal nature that we came from and the eternal nature we return to. We know that there is never an end and never a goodbye. We will experience changes, never losses. We are changing, we are never losing. All of our journey can be enjoyable. It will not be without difficult situations because those situations serve to provide us with contrast and challenges for us to decide who we are and who we want to be. We begin to look at situations differently and in that different perspective, we become a light to others in a world that can sometimes have darkness.

We work our lives, our thoughts, and our reactions in a way that will help us feel the best we can in any situation. When we ascribe to the theories that, "All is Well," and "This too shall Pass" we give ourselves a power that we would not otherwise experience. We begin to live deliberately, creating the life we want, not the life we get by default. We direct our thoughts and feelings in a way that will give us what we ask for. We "get out of our own way" and allow the Universe, Source, or God, to give us that which we truly want. The more our feelings match those of love and appreciation, the more quickly we will receive what we have asked for.

Magic truly happens when we live a life that we deliberately create. We will be in balance, and we will know that whatever is happening and where ever our life stands at the time is exactly where it needs to be for us to realize our dreams. In the knowing, the appreciation for everything, regardless, we open up ourselves to experience that Nirvana state that seems so often to elude us. Others look at us and see only light and beauty. We live in a way that draws to us all the good things in life that we are striving for. We come from within, from the soul rather than the ego. We do not place ourselves in a place of superiority or inferiority, we place ourselves firmly where we are and we accept that place. We rejoice in the days of rain as well as the days of sunshine. We know that we cannot experience rainbows without rain. We cannot appreciate the vistas from the mountains unless we have passed through the valleys. It all works together for our good.

We think of the Universe and the magnificence of all of creation as a gift for us. We realize that it is in the creating that the Universe experiences itself and we understand that we are needed. If we were not here, a void would be created. We have a power, a presence, that causes the Universe to expand and it is in that expansion that all of creation takes place. We know that God cannot be divided, and if God cannot be divided then we understand that we are an extension of that God power, of that God of creation. It is within us to create. That is why we are here.

What will you create? When you answer that question and live your life in a way that creates your best self, you will be achieving your purpose during this incarnation. Everyone has a purpose, a calling, a dharma. Some individuals exhibit such a presence that they are known worldwide, sometimes in a positive way and sometimes not so positive. Keep in mind, however that the contrast between what we call "good" and "bad" is simply a value scale so that we can decide how we want to live our lives. It is only when the observation of a situation causes you to feel badly that you will realize an imbalance. Ten people can observe the same scene and four of them may not find a problem with the situation. For those four people, this causes them no distress because the situation fits in with what keeps them in balance. The other six may find problems to a different extent and that will give them a contrast that will lead to a decision about their life. This is how we continually create and recreate our best self. We make these decisions daily and in the making of the decisions that make us feel good, we remain in balance.

The course is called our life. We journey along, and it is when we discover our Godpower and our ability to deliberately create that we understand the true meaning of our source energy. When this happens, we are in balance. Always. We know that what we perceive as imbalance is yet another opportunity to observe the contrast and make a decision on how we will react. In that reaction, we create our future circumstances. We will do this deliberately, or by default, but we are the creators of our life.

This is the information that was shared in "The Secret", the information shared by many authors, and the information shared by Jesus when he told us, "....whoever believes in me will do the works I have been doing and they will do even greater things than these." We have been given many teachers in many different times and from many different places to help us on our journey. Search your heart and your soul and choose those tools that will help you become your very best self daily.

Namaste and love to you all.